COUNTRY SUNSHINE
The Dottie West Story

Judy Berryhill & Frances Meeker

EGGMAN PUBLISHING

Editor:
  Melanie A. Plesce

Jacket design:
  Mike Walker

Design, typography, and text production:
  TypeByte Graphix

Library of Congress: 94-62009

ISBN: 1-886371-08-3

Eggman Publishing
3012 Hedrick Street
Nashville, Tennessee 37203
1-800-396-4626

*To all of Dottie's fans
whom she loved
and respected so
deeply throughout
her singing career.*

Judy Berryhill

*To Orville, who
always believed I
could write a book.*

Frances Meeker

Table
of
Contents

Acknowledgement

All the wonderful people who so kindly and graciously helped out with the preparation of this book turned our task into enjoyment. It would be impossible to mention here all those who, in one way or another, furnished important information, but, we are grateful to all.

Charlie, Willie and Jay — for being great breakfast buddies.

Bill Berryhill — made endless trips driving us everywhere we needed to go. He was always there when we needed him.

Jean Cashion — when we needed computer typing done, she never turned us down.

Richard Cashion — for his time and endless hours driving to take pictures for this book.

Jack Jones—remembering many things of Dottie's younger life that we had forgotten.

Sue Carter—for all her phone calls, letters and information she contributed. Her memories have indeed made this a better book.

Joe Bob Basham—for sharing his recollections of when he and Dottie were in the Coonskins band during high school.

Addadean Morgan Glenn—had many memories of Dottie since they played together as children and went to grammar and high school together.

Bertlan Glenn—recalled many interesting things of the Marsh family and had gone all the way through school with Dottie.

Dot Davis—just being there as a friend when we needed her.

Ralph Klank—for sharing his impressions of the Marsh family and allowing us to walk through his cattle pastures to the house where Dottie once lived with her family when she was in high school.

To all the wonderful people at the courthouses and libraries in Smithville and McMinnville for all their work and information they furnished.

O N E

Ghosts

A generation's fate was set one summer night in 1912 when a young mother tucked her four-year-old son, Hollis, and his sister, three-year-old Elsie, into their beds. She kissed them goodbye and walked out of their room and out of their lives.

Weeks passed with no word from their young mother, Minnie. Ruben Marsh had given up hope of his wife ever returning. If he ever knew why she left, he never once mentioned it. Neighbors and friends helped care for the children while he worked as a barber in his Huntsville, Alabama shop. When absolutely all hope of his wife's returning had faded, he felt he had no choice but send Elsie to live with relatives. Hollis was left to grow up on the streets, fending for himself.

Hollis dwelled deeply on what could have happened to his mother all the while missing his sister terribly. Each night while he tried to sleep, terror filled his thoughts. He secretly feared that his daddy would leave, too. As the days passed into weeks, Hollis fell asleep each night on a tear-stained pillow.

The five years Hollis attended school was especially hard on him. It wasn't that he could not comprehend the material being taught. He just felt the missing link in his life too deeply.

"Jealousy and concealed rage often turned to tears when other parents would come to school to be with their children," he once said. "But as time passed, I learned to hide my tears."

Hollis began skipping school and finally dropped out, never to return. He exchanged his education for playing marbles with other boys who also did not attend school. Unfortunately, a few years later, the marble games were exchanged for drinking and staying out late. The years did little to diminish the hurt of losing his mother and sister, something he would never be able to forget. "It was as if a master welder used his torch and burned that scene deeply into my memory," he once confessed.

Hollis' adult life became marked by violence and tragedy. His wife and children knew poverty, abuse, and incest. "But you have to remember that Hollis himself suffered rejection and neglect," said Anna Mannon, a sister of the Tennessee girl whom Hollis married. "Our family always tried to understand what made him like he was."

When Hollis was twenty-two, he left Huntsville to visit an uncle who lived in DeKalb County in Middle Tennessee. His uncle drove a school wagon pulled by two large mules, taking children from the rural area to Belk School. All of the young people called him Uncle Ardle. Unlike the man Hollis was eventually to become, Uncle Ardle was a kind and gentle soul who would do anything for a neighbor. The children loved him dearly.

Later on, Uncle Ardle replaced the school wagon with a large yellow school bus. On Sundays, he also used the bus to carry the neighbors, who did not have cars, to church. "I will never forget what a great person he was," a neighbor said.

One afternoon, Hollis went with Uncle Ardle on the school round. Among the students getting on the wagon was sixteen-year-old Pelina Artha Jones. Hollis was smitten by her olive complexion, a trait she inherited from her paternal grandmother, a Cherokee Indian.

Pelina was the daughter of Bill Jones, a large landowner in the Belk Community, and Margaret, Bill's second wife. Bill's first wife, Louisa, died on December 11, 1911, from typhoid fever, leaving Bill with nine children. Two years later Bill met Margaret France and twelve months later they were married. Together they had eleven children, making him the father of twenty children. Pelina was Bill and Margaret's first child. In the year 1931, Bill was sixty-four when his last children, twins, were born.

On the bus Pelina was attracted to the young man with wavy black hair and blue eyes, but her parents were unapproving. However, Hollis soon began courting Pelina at her parents' home, which was only a mile from Uncle Ardle's, where Hollis was staying. "When I first laid eyes on her, I knew she would be the girl I would marry," Hollis said years later.

Pelina was somewhat resentful because she was allowed to date only on Saturday nights and Sunday afternoons, and the dates could be conducted only at her parents' home. "You're not going to be roaming the countryside with a t-total stranger," was her mother's response when Pelina would complain about the situation.

When Pelina explained to Hollis that she could not go out with him in his car, he was downright contemptible. He did not take to these arrangements very lightly but there was nothing he could do, so he and Pelina looked forward to Saturday nights when they would listen to the radio together. A country music show, the Grand Ole Opry, originating in Nashville about seventy-five miles away, was broadcast through WSM radio into homes across the country every Saturday night.

The Grand Ole Opry, which was first broadcast on the air November 28, 1925, would become world famous, but was then only seven years old. In the beginning, the Grand Ole Opry was originally known as the Saturday Night Barn Dance. The country music performance followed a program of opera, symphonic and light classical music called the Music Appreciation Hour.

In the depression-ridden South, the lives of many people were brightened considerably on those Saturday nights. The performers included Uncle Dave Macon, who was billed as the Dixie Dewdrop, the Gully Jumpers, the Dixie Clodhoppers, Sam and Kirk McGee, and Texas Ruby Fox.

Initially, the Grand Ole Opry had been broadcast from the WSM radio studio, which was housed and owned by National Life and Accident Insurance Company. As the country music show gained popularity, fans began crowding into the WSM corridors to get a glimpse of their favorite performers, so National Life built a 500-seat observation studio so fans could watch the performance. Still the crowds grew, so the show was moved to a theater, and later to Nashville's War Memorial Building, which could seat 3,000 people.

Hollis was no longer content just to listen to the radio with Pelina, and he soon began pressing her for marriage. Her parents, of course, objected. It was plain to Bill and Margaret that Hollis would never fit in with the Jones family. Unlike Hollis, the Joneses were a hard-working family. Pelina's father was at the barn with her brothers every morning before daybreak, hitching up the mules by lantern light. They were in the fields before sunrise. Meanwhile, her mother and sisters spent the days cooking, cleaning, and doing laundry for the large family. The women also planted two large gardens every summer. Hollis, though, was unemployed with no direction in his life. Occasionally, he repaired cars and watches, but he never held a steady job.

Yet, the boy who had grown up on the streets of Huntsville knew how to go after what he wanted. He told Pelina that if she did not marry him, he would kill her and her parents, as well as burn down their house. Pelina, as young and inexperienced as she was, believed him. Within a week, she had convinced her parents that marriage was the right thing for her. Sadly, they gave in, afraid she would run away from home if they refused.

Hollis and Pelina were married by the Justice of the Peace in Smithville, the county seat of DeKalb County, fourteen miles away, on October 30, 1931. Little did they know that the once-abandoned little boy would become the father of a baby girl who would become the internationally-known country music singer and Grand Ole Opry Star — Dottie West.

T W O

Seeds of Sorrow

The newlyweds moved into an old house in Bain Hollow about a half mile from Pelina's former home. The cabin was of a typical Southern pioneer structure with two rooms on each side of an open hallway, commonly called a "dog trot." The family dogs slept there, joined by their owners in the summertime because of the cool breeze that was always blowing. The owner of the house allowed the young couple to live there for free, as long as they did not damage the property.

Pelina's father obtained some lumber from his sawmill and made the couple some tables and chairs. Her mother made a bedtick filled with fresh straw for their mattress. She also made two goose-down pillows. She gave them some of her linens and quilts along with dishes and cooking utensils.

Hollis and Pelina were completely preoccupied with their young love and surroundings. They gave little thought to tomorrow. However, on Saturday nights they missed listening to the Grand Ole Opry. The only thing they had to listen to was the night sounds in the hollow that consisted of crickets, owls and the large bull frogs on the banks of the Caney Branch.

A short time later, Hollis scouted up a broken second-hand radio, and with a little tinkering to its parts, the Opry could be heard loud and clear.

Neighbors and relatives described Hollis, or 'Ollis, as some pronounced his name, as a mechanical genius. He could take a car battery, scrap lumber, and a few pieces of metal and rig up mechanical plows to turn the land for a garden. With odd pieces of wood and metal, he could rig up a crude water wheel and pump to bring water from the creek into the back yard of the house.

Once he took a speedometer gear from a car and used it to power the hand clippers that Pelina used to cut the hair of the family and neighbors. He was much sought after to repair watches and clocks in the neighborhood.

At first, Pelina was genuinely happy with her marriage. But as the weeks went by, her blissfulness began to fade. She began to realize the truth that her parents had tried to instill in her. Nevertheless, she found some comfort in knowing that she might have saved their lives.

Pelina had to learn to be frugal with food, because the couple rarely had much. Hollis became verbally abusive when what little they did have ran out. So, she often went to her parents' home for lunch while Hollis was away. Yet, she dared not let him know what she was doing. He very seldom visited his in-laws because he was uncomfortable with their lifestyle, which included going to church every Sunday.

In desperation, Pelina meekly suggested that Hollis find a job in Smithville or Mc-Minnville. He was so infuriated that he knocked her down and kicked her. She never mentioned it again. Often she thought about leaving and filing for divorce, yet divorces were a rarity in the 30s. In addition, Hollis' threat weighed heavily on her. She realized that she had disappointed her parents by getting married too young and to the wrong man; therefore, she had no intentions of adding to their pain.

Meanwhile, the scarcity of food at the Marsh cabin was forcing Pelina to climb the steep hill to her parents' home more frequently. Although Hollis never joined her, Margaret always sent Pelina home with enough food for Hollis' supper. His hunger kept him from punishing Pelina. Yet young Pelina never told her family of her abuse. Margaret thought Pelina had not yet mastered the techniques of cooking and attributed that to Pelina's hearty appetite.

In the dead of winter, Hollis set up a distillery in one of the two empty rooms across the open hallway. He began making moonshine whiskey from fermented corn mash and creek water. He used what little money he had to buy sugar for his illegal product. However, he enjoyed the whiskey so much, that he never made enough to sell for a profit.

Pelina learned that she was pregnant in the middle of January. While Hollis was elated by the news, Pelina was worried. "We should have waited until we were more financially able to start a family," she argued. "Aw, shucks," Hollis, with little concern, replied. "Don't worry about that; everything will be alright."

And that was the end of it. Pelina's fear of her husband forced her to try to forget her financial woes. *Maybe Hollis is going to get a job he hasn't told me about,* she frequently thought to herself.

But as spring faded into summer, Hollis had hardly made enough money from his pitiful jobs to buy their food. They went to bed hungry on many nights; yet Pelina still did not tell her parents of their suffering. Although she had walked away from the only real love she ever knew and was trapped in a loveless marriage, Pelina still put up a good front when she visited her family.

Not realizing Pelina was being untruthful, her parents began to think Hollis was doing better in his job, and they continued to send the couple food when Pelina was due to deliver her first child and unable to visit them. Pelina tried whatever she could to ease the burden. With a hoe, she attempted to dig a garden, yet the weeds overtook every inch she cultivated. The smoldering summer weather was no help.

"Hollis never made any attempt to get a full-time job. At times he was almost unbearable to be near, especially when he was drunk. Often, he abused and beat me for no reason at all," Pelina once told her aunt years later. "There were times he would leave in late morning, driving that old A-Model up that long steep hill. He would never say where he was going. And I wished so many times that he would never come back. But sometime after dark, that old car could be heard for miles away, roaring back into the hollow. Then there were days when he would never leave the house."

Gradually, all the fear within her overshadowed all the love that she had ever felt for Hollis. But when Hollis was home, she pretended nothing had changed. At times Pelina could detect a flicker of love from him, but it never lasted long.

On the morning of October 10, 1932, Hollis sat in the open hallway, playing his fiddle while Pelina was walking along Caney Branch looking for hickory nuts. She disturbed a bumblebee in the wildflowers along the bank, and, realizing her mistake, began to run back to the cabin. Just as she reached the front yard, she stumbled over the root of a tree and fell to the ground. Hollis continued to play his fiddle, even chuckling at his wife's predicament. Pelina picked herself up and made her way into the cabin.

The next morning at four o'clock, Dorothy Marie Marsh was born.

PLACE OF BIRTH
Co. or _Dekalb_

STATE OF TENNESSEE
STATE DEPARTMENT OF HEALTH
DIVISION OF VITAL STATISTICS

37365

CERTIFICATE OF BIRTH

Dist. _____
Town _Smithville_ Registration District No. _215_   File No. _____
Primary Registration Dist. No. _4210_ Registered No. _135_

(No. _____ St. _____ Ward _____
(If birth occured in a hospital or institution, give its NAME instead of street and number)

NAME OF CHILD _Dorothy Diane Marsh_
If child is not yet named, make supplemental report, as directed

| If Plural births | Twin, triplet, or other _____ | 6. Premature _No_ | Legitimate? _yes_ | 8. Date of Birth _Oct 11_ _1932_ |
| | 5. Number, in order of birth _____ | Full term _yes_ | | Month, day, year |

FATHER _Hollis Marsh_ 620

18. Full maiden name **MOTHER** _Edna Jones_

(usual place of abode)
resident, give place and State) _____

19. Residence (usual place of abode)
(If nonresident, give place and State) _____

11. Race _W_ 12. Age at last birthday _24_ (years)

20. Color or race _W_ 21. Age at last birthday _17_ (years)

(city or place country) _Smithville_

22. Birthplace (city or place)
(State or country) _Smithville_

profession, or particular
work done, as spinner,
Bookkeeper, etc. _Farmer_

23. Trade, profession, or particular kind of work done, as housekeeper, typist, nurse, clerk, etc. _House work_

se business in which
was done, as silk mill
bank, etc. _____

24. Industry or business in which work was done, as own home, lawyer's office, silk mill, etc. _____

month and year last
in this work _____

25. Date (month and year) last engaged in this work _____ 19___

17. Total time (years)
_____ spent in this work

26. Total time (years) _____ spent in this work

children born to this mother, including this child _0_
born alive but now dead _0_

(a) Total number now living _____
(c) Total number stillborn _____
(d) Born at full term _0_

___ Months
or weeks   29. Cause of stillbirth

Before labor _____
During labor _____

CERTIFICATE OF ATTENDING PHYSICIAN OR MIDWIFE

that I attended the birth of this child, who was _alive_ _____ on the date above stated.
(Born alive or stillborn)

the attending physician
the father, householder,
this return.

(Signed) _Dr. Allen_ M.D.
or _____ Midwife

added from a
report _____

20 January (Date of)

Address _Smithville_
Filed _10-10-1932_

Registrar

T H R E E

This Too Shall Pass

Thirty years later, little Dorothy Marie, born in that old cabin, would become Dottie West, the well-known country music star, award-winning songwriter, television performer, and movie actress.

Pelina now was no longer the only one forced to experience Hollis' abuse. The tiny baby was keeping her parents up at nights with colic, the severe abdominal pains that often plague newborn babies. One evening Pelina was rocking the crying baby when Hollis returned home drunk, as usual. He became enraged and yanked the child from her mother's arms, giving her a hard spanking.

During that winter, the only gravel road leading out of Bain Hollow became iced over, inhibiting Pelina's family to visit for weeks.

While she missed her family very much, she mostly longed to hear their laughter again. She was afraid she would forget how to laugh, so, at times, she stood in front of a small mirror and practiced. Often her laughter would turn to tears. At home alone much of the time with only the baby, she was forced to take an ax into the woods and chop wood to keep a fire going in the two rooms. Little Dorothy was left alone on a pallet on the floor.

After a long hard winter, spring finally arrived. With Dorothy in her arms, Pelina began to scout for blackberry blooms. She climbed the steep hill behind the cabin and discovered that the beautiful white blooms were in abundance. She then realized that her small family would not go hungry that summer.

Two months later, the berries still hung heavily on the bushes. While Dorothy was napping, Pelina again climbed the hill, returning with a gallon of the fruit. She cleaned and washed the berries, which filled two large bowls. One bowl would be for their supper and the other one for their breakfast.

Later that day, Pelina took Dorothy to her parents' home. Since it was Friday, a day when Hollis often staggered in rather late, she asked her mother if her sisters America and Susie could spend the night with her so she wouldn't have to go home to an empty house.

"Where do you think they would sleep? You only have one bed," her mother asked.

"I will make them a pallet," Pelina quickly replied.

After some consideration, Pelina's mother allowed Susie to go. However, she said, she needed America to stay home to help with the younger children.

The next morning, their breakfast consisted only of blackberries, which had sat in the kitchen all night. Pelina had falsely told her sister that Hollis forgot to buy sugar, so the berries had to be eaten without any. While unsweetened berries were unfamiliar to Susie, she pretended she enjoyed them to appease her sister.

While they were eating, Hollis sat across from Pelina, putting berries in his spoon and flinging them at her. Pelina was afraid to ask him to stop, and by the time he did, her face, hair, and clothes were covered with blackberry juice.

Even though Pelina told Susie that Hollis was just showing off because of her visit, it was years before Susie made another trip to her sister's home. She always made up some excuse when asked to visit. She just could not bear to see her sister mistreated.

Through the years, no matter how hard Susie tried to forget that visit, it would never fade from her mind.

By the time Dorothy reached her first birthday, Hollis was whipping her on a regular basis. Afterwards he would tease-whip her and make her laugh. But there was one soothing and uniting force in the cabin — music. Hollis played his fiddle every day, and Pelina, who had a voice admired by her family and friends, sang and yodeled the ballads that generations of her family had sung.

Hollis knew the songs of Jimmy Rodgers, the famed father of commercial country music, who died of tuberculosis in 1933 at the height of his career. Hollis could play such Rodgers' tunes as "TB Blues," "T for Texas," and "Muleskinner Blues."

At the age of two, Dorothy was finding the voice that would enable Dottie West to become a pioneer in establishing females as solo singing stars and songwriters during the days when Nashville would become famous as Music City.

Yet with the coming of winter, even music could not ease the burden of the Marsh family. As a last resort, Pelina, at long last, made her way up the hill to her parents' home and told them of her food shortage. However, she neglected to mention that she was again pregnant.

Shortly thereafter, the Marshes moved in with Pelina's family. While Hollis objected at first, he relented, realizing that there was no other choice. On the other hand, though, he enjoyed the bountiful meals Pelina's mother cooked three times a day.

The time had come when Pelina had to tell her mother about the new baby on the way. Meanwhile, little Dorothy was basking in the love and attention of her grandparents, uncles, aunts, and cousins. She quickly learned by watching the twins, who were only one year older than herself. Each night after they ate their supper, all three happily followed their granddaddy into the family room. They climbed on his lap and he would sing his made-up song.

"You're my little Bodgin Boy and Bougin Girl." He would sing the song over and over again while rocking them. That was an every-night customary thing for them to do. Often, Margaret would lift the sleeping children from his arms and lay them in bed without even arousing them. But for Dorothy, this did not last long. Through the years, she thought her granddaddy was the greatest man on earth.

Bill and Margaret did not know about Hollis' drinking, and Pelina was now both ashamed and afraid to tell them. She knew he was hiding his whiskey jug in the bushes away from the house, because she saw him sneak out periodically to take a nip.

Despite his disapproval of the man, Bill told Hollis of the house he wanted to build for the Marsh family on the land across the road. All he asked of Hollis was that he help with the construction. Hollis unenthusiastically agreed.

A few weeks after the birth of Dorothy's brother, Oza Ollendroff, on May 28, 1934, Bill and his sons had hauled enough lumber from the sawmill to begin building the house. But Hollis balked on his agreement to help with the construction. He told Pelina that he needed to visit his father in Huntsville. She suggested that she accompany him to Alabama so she and the children could meet their paternal grandfather. Hollis, however, refused.

The house was nearly finished when Hollis returned from Alabama three weeks later.

The Marsh family could move into their new home in just a few days.

Early the next morning, Hollis sneaked out to have a nip of his whiskey. Unable to find it in the weeds and bushes, he stormed back into the house, cursing and threatening everyone. He retrieved his gun from his bedroom and confronted Bill and Margaret when they rushed to the hallway to see what the commotion was. "You got my whiskey!" Hollis yelled at his father-in-law. He then aimed the pistol at Bill's head and pulled the trigger. The pistol clicked, but did not fire. In his rage, Hollis had forgotten to load it. Margaret jumped between Bill and Hollis, only to have her front teeth knocked out by the pistol butt.

Awakened by the racket, the children were coming out of their rooms into the hall, except for three-year-old Dorothy, who crawled under a bed.

Bill demanded Hollis to leave and never come back. However, he told Pelina that she and the children always had a home there.

Hollis turned to Pelina with rage in his eyes. He ordered Pelina to gather the two children and what little clothing they had. The sorrowful Jones family watched them drive off. The next week Bill and his sons finished construction of the house across the road, in hope that Pelina and the children would return.

Hollis rented a two-room house in the Greenhills community in Warren County, halfway between Smithville and McMinnville. He borrowed a truck and then went back to the cabin in Bain Hollow to retrieve his abandoned furniture. Later that night, he sneaked back to the almost-finished house across from Pelina's parents, poured gasoline on the structure, and struck a match. He later told someone that if he could not live in that house, no one could.

During the next year, Hollis refused to allow Pelina to visit her family, whom she missed very much. She briefly entertained the idea of walking the fifteen miles to Bill and Margaret's home, but she was again pregnant. Despite this, Pelina's weight had dropped below one hundred pounds. Hollis was still not providing for his family.

The radio was Pelina's only companion. During the day, she seldom turned it off. She listened to Kitty Wells, country music's first major female solo star, who was broadcast by radio station WXIX in Nashville in 1936 with her husband, Johnny Wright, and his sister.

To Pelina, what seemed like two of the happiest voices on the air belonged to Lulu Belle and Scotty Wiseman. They had been married for two years, and their marriage was still bubbling over with love. When one of their songs came on, Pelina always turned the radio up a little louder. Pelina's own sorrow was forgotten when she listened to the happiness of others.

Hollis often went back to DeKalb County to see his friend, Ben West. One day Hollis came home riding a motorcycle. It looked like it was ready for the junkyard, just like everything else he brought home. Hollis wanted Pelina to go for a ride with him. She glanced out of the window. "Hollis, it's getting late and colder. It will be dark in a little while," she said.

"Don't worry about that. We are just going up the road a little ways and right back," he promised her.

"Well, OK but let me put the babies to bed first."

"Make it snappy," he said as he went out the door. Quickly, she tucked the three small children all in one bed and told Dorothy to keep them in bed.

Instead of Hollis taking her just a short distance, he went back down to Ben West's place, near Rankhorn Hill. Hollis wanted to show off his motorcycle to his buddy, Ben. Meanwhile, Pelina was worried about her children.

As darkness settled in, they got back on the motorcycle to return home. Hollis tried his best, but the motorcycle would not turn over. Ben offered to take them home, but his car had frozen up because he had forgotten to drain the water out of it the night before. Hollis and Pelina had no choice but to stay overnight. Pelina did not close her eyes all night for worrying and thinking her babies would freeze to death. By daybreak the next morning, Hollis was working on the motorcycle. Within the hour they were ready to leave for home.

When they arrived, Pelina jumped off of the motorcycle and ran into the house ahead of Hollis.

Dorothy had put caps and coats on all of them. Luckily, the children had survived the ice-cold house without catching a sniffle.

Pelina anxiously waited for spring to arrive. There was a small, but rich, garden plot in the back yard. She asked a neighbor if she could borrow a hoe to dig up the soil.

"Mrs. Marsh, it will take more than a hoe

to loosen that ground. I will plow your garden for you tomorrow when I plow my own," he said.

The neighbors had already observed what kind of man Hollis was. One gave Pelina a hoe and told her to keep it. Through the years she protected that hoe as if it were made of gold.

During that summer, five-year-old Dorothy very seldom got to go out and play. She had to bathe the babies and diaper them during the day. She swept the floors and washed the dishes. Her beautiful natural curls usually hung limp from being in the sweltering cabin all day.

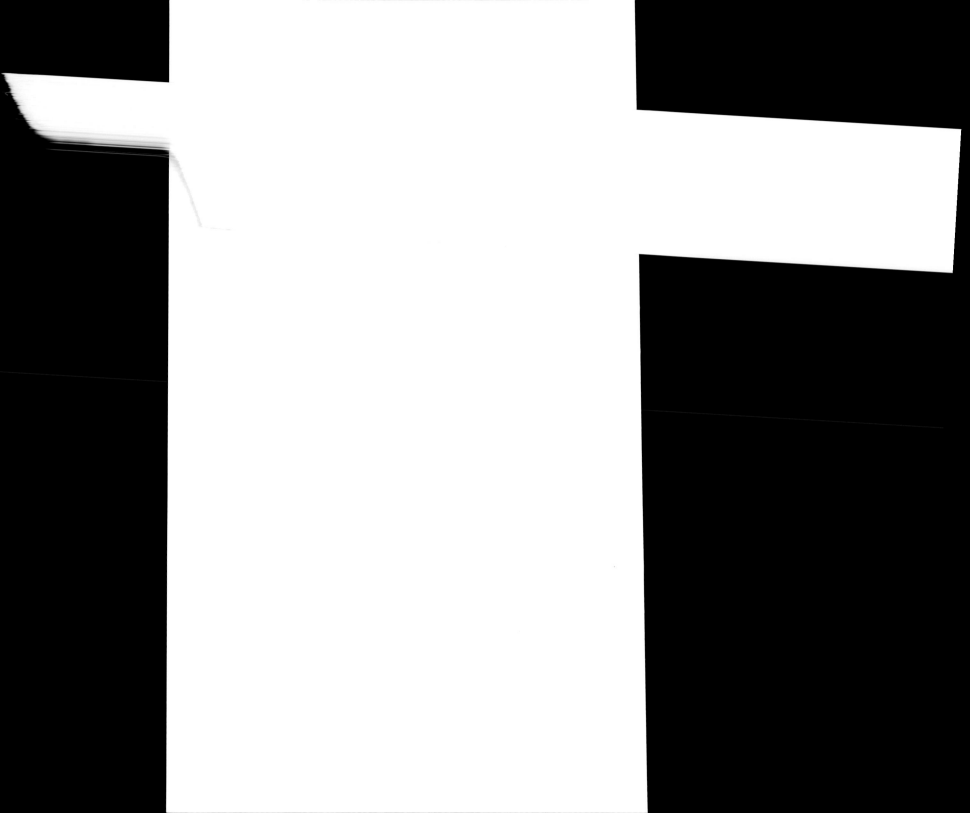

FO

Darknes

By the time Dorothy was five years old, three more children had been born.

Hollis moved his family into another two-room house, the Ervin House, in the Moore's College Community, which was only a mile from the home of Pelina's twenty-three-year-old sister, Melvina "Vina" Turner.

If that house had not been protected by large trees and deep forest, the storms would have blown it down years ago. There were no screen windows or doors, and the cracks in the floors were so wide that if the children dropped anything, it usually landed on the ground. They quickly learned to hold onto a piece of bread.

When Pelina spotted rain clouds in the sky, she began setting buckets under leaks

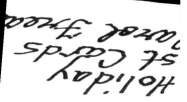

to catch the rain. Her beds had buckets sitting on them as well.

During the summer, there was always an abundance of fresh air coming through the cracks in the walls. It made sleeping comfortable. However, she awoke one night to feel a snake crawling over her. After that, she would get up several times during the night to check on her children, being afraid that a snake would bite them or choke them to death.

Back then, Dorothy was afraid of the dark. One night when Hollis was in one of his drunken stupors, he became irritated with Dorothy and made her sleep on the porch. Pelina wanted to bring her in when they were ready for bed but Hollis dared not let her. He then threw an old quilt out on the porch for her to lie on. When Hollis went to sleep, Pelina took two pillows and went out on the porch and slept with Dorothy.

As children, Dorothy and her brother Oza's favorite thing to do was climbing trees — not the large trees, but the smaller ones that had many small limbs. But their parents had warned them over and over to never climb trees. They had explained to them how easily they could fall and get hurt. One evening, Hollis came home only to find both Dorothy and Oza up in a tree. His temper raged out of control. The children immediately started down the tree but Hollis ordered them to stay where they were. He ran into the house and grabbed the first thing he saw, a birdseye diaper. As he rushed out of the door, he was ripping it into strips. Pelina ran to the door, wondering what Hollis was up to. She could not imagine what would make him tear up a diaper, which had long ago become a shortage in their home. Quickly, he climbed the tree and tied Dorothy and Oza's hands and feet to the tree limbs. The children were too frightened to cry, but as darkness fell, their moaning cries were easily heard from inside. It was near midnight before Hollis let them down. Never again did they climb a tree.

Bill and Margaret worried about their daughter and grandchildren, but still did not know the full extent of what Pelina and her children were going through. Besides, they were deeply concerned about their daughter, Vina and were spending a lot of time visiting her. Sadly, Vina had contracted tuberculosis.

When spring came, they carried Vina

home with them to spend the summer. Vina was then unable to be up for more than a few minutes at a time. During the day, she lay on a cot in the open hall where a cool breeze soothed her feverish body.

Kermit, Vina's husband, had kept their three small boys home where his mother helped care for them. During the day, Margaret kept the younger children outdoors away from Vina. She wanted to protect them from the dreaded disease if she possibly could. In the woods, they made playhouses, swung on grapevines and waded in the cool branch. The older children were always busy helping with chores. Margaret spent a lot of time with her daughter. She knew that if anyone came down with the disease, it would probably be she. She kept everything as clean and sterile as she possibly could.

But as the summer drifted into fall, Vina was thinking more of her family. Only a few times had Kermit brought the boys to see her. He was afraid they too would come down with TB. Bill had tried, unsuccessfully, to find a doctor who would know what to do for his daughter. Finally, he realized his daughter was doomed for death.

"Mother, I want to go home to die," Vina said weakly to her.

TB was widespread, and most families were touched by it in some way.

These families could relate to that song that Jimmy Rodgers was singing on the radio, "TB Blues," with its hard truth.

> *I've been fighting like a lion,*
> *Looks like I'm going to lose,*
> *'cause there ain't nobody*
> *Ever whipped the TB blues.*

In those years, there was no medication for the disease that was marked by a dry, hacking cough, fever, night sweats, and weight loss. Doctors would prescribe bed rest, sun baths and a diet of raw eggs and milk.

The family had heard of a new TB hospital in Nashville on Ben Allen Road. After checking into it, they found its purpose was mainly to take patients in to keep them from spreading the disease to other family members. After talking about this to Vina, they decided that at home, surrounded by her loved ones, was the place for her to die. That afternoon, Bill did not bother the farmers who had cars. He knew they were busy gathering their corn and hay. He filled a wagon bed with straw and placed a featherbed on top. Margaret spread quilts and sheets over the featherbed making a bed for Vina's final ride home.

Bill and Margaret now were caring for two daughters who could not care for themselves. They were carrying food to both families. To Vina's because there was no one to prepare food at her home, and to Pelina's because she had very little food in her house.

Every day, weather permitting, Pelina walked the long miles through the field to see her sick sister. She would leave Dorothy, now eight years old, at home to watch over the younger children. But by the first of December, Pelina, who was pregnant again, often felt she could not walk the distance after caring for, and doing laundry on a washboard for a family of seven. On those days when she could not make the trip, she would send Dorothy and Oza. "Only stay one hour and tell Aunt Vina you love her. Tell Mammy to let you know when your hour is up," she would say as they went out the door.

Dorothy's love for her aunt had no boundaries. Oza loved his aunt but, nevertheless, his mind was more on the shiny red wagon outside that needed someone to play with. Oza looked forward to playing with Vina's three young boys. But most of the time, Kermit kept the boys at his mother's, who lived nearby.

During the last weeks of Vina's life, Margaret stayed with her day and night. Tommy, her brother, was called in from the service. Even though the leaders of the armed forces might have seemed strict on their soldiers, they still had compassion for them during a time of illness and death back home.

F I V E

Lost Hope

It was 1943 and the world's most famous country music show had outgrown its theatre. Their new location was at the Ryman Auditorium, located a block off of Broadway and five blocks from the Cumberland River.

The red brick building with the steep roof, had originated as the Union Gospel Tabernacle built in 1890 by Captain Tom Ryman. It was constructed at a cost of $100,000, most of which came from Ryman's own pocket. Ryman was also the owner of six Cumberland River steamboats and had become the prize convert of the great evangelist of that day, Sam Jones. Jones, a recovering alcoholic, had come to Nashville in 1885 and held a revival at Tulip Street Methodist Church in the old Edgefield area across the river from downtown.

Back in 1890, an estimated 5,000 people filled the new tabernacle on its opening night. At the big revival of 1898, 15,000 people tried to get into the building. Hundreds were converted and thousands of men vowed to abstain from liquor and gambling.

In addition to Jones, some of the most famous American preachers of that day filled the pulpit of the tabernacle. When Tom Ryman died in 1905, Sam Jones held the funeral there and proposed that the building be named the "Ryman Auditorium." Jones died a year later.

As revivalism waned in Nashville and throughout the country, the Ryman Auditorium, under trustee ownership, became the cultural center of Nashville. Its bookings were some of the greatest opera companies, symphonies, and theater casts in the world. But that era, too, came to an end, leaving the Ryman empty, until the move of the Grand Ole Opry.

The popularity of the Grand Ole Opry spread to Americans who were not otherwise familiar with it. Opry performers began to make personal appearances at military bases, both in the states and abroad.

Despite the war, the Ryman Auditorium was always packed. The streets of Nashville were filled with cars from nearly every state, as well as Canada. Canadian license plates became a familiar sight on the Nashville streets.

The terrible attack on Pearl Harbor in 1941 had thrown the country and the world into war. But it had scarcely touched the Marsh family in their isolated home in Warren County. There were some friends and relatives who went into the military service, but Hollis, who was now making a little money working on cars in his yard, was not among them.

It was near the end of the war when Hollis was drafted into service. Pelina and her family were not ashamed to admit to one another that they looked upon his military induction as a blessing to the family. The government allotment checks for dependents brought them more money than they had ever seen.

His leaving quieted old terrors for Dorothy. As a young child, Hollis had begun secretly molesting her, relying on threats to silence her. Her acute fear of him was only outweighed by the promises of doom for her and those around her. But to her mother nothing was ever said.

It was only weeks away from the Easter Parade and egg hunt at Moore's College. Dorothy so desperately wanted a new dress to wear on the special occasion. Pelina weighed the situation very carefully before buying the dress. It was a bright yellow dress, trimmed in red ricrac. It cost $1.49. For years Dorothy told everybody how expensive her dress was.

Yet their blessings were short-lived. Hollis was discharged from the Marine Corps within three months. As for the reason, Pelina simply told her mother that the government probably thought Hollis was not worth the big allotment check that was going to his family.

Pelina was able to save enough from the allotment checks to buy one acre of land near the place they were then living. The land was secluded far back into the woods. She had also saved enough to buy the lumber to build a house.

By spring, Pelina was pregnant again. In spite of that, she worked right along beside Hollis in building the house. She lifted and handed up the long planks to him, high upon a ladder, as he nailed them on. When it was time to put the roof on, being seven months pregnant didn't stop her. She climbed that ladder and nailed as many shingles on as Hollis did. The children cleared the area of rocks and broken tree limbs. The entire family was proud that at last they had a home of their own and one that did not have a leaky roof like their other houses.

The whole family was elated. Eleven-year-old Dorothy was excited because she thought she might have a room of her own. But as it turned out, she had to share her room which was on one end of the small attic with a sister and two brothers. Their little room was furnished with two beds, a small table and a cardboard box to hold their clothes. The children had to climb to their room by boards nailed to the wall beneath the hole cut through the ceiling of the downstairs. The hole was barely large enough for them to squeeze through.

Downstairs was a front room furnished with two beds and a few other pieces of furniture. A lean-to kitchen was in the back of the house.

There were no toilet facilities, but Pelina was careful to observe propriety by instructing the girls to use the woods on the left of the house and the boys to go the right. Dorothy and her sisters kept a playhouse in the girl's area of the woods so the boys would not disturb them. Soon after they moved in, Dorothy carved her name on an oak tree in front of the house in letters that are still visible fifty years later.

The attic was divided into two rooms. Hollis used the other room for his watch repair shop. He gave strict orders that no one could go into that room. Many nights when Pelina thought he was working on watches, he had Dorothy in there, raping her. She was too scared to ever tell her mother. No matter how painful, he ordered her never to make a sound. There were times during the day, especially on rainy days when he could not be outside working on cars, that he pretended to be working on watches. Shortly after he went in there, he would call downstairs saying he had dropped a tiny screw and needed Dorothy to help him find it. Dorothy knew what she was in for when she heard her name being called. He gave her orders to tell her mother that she found the tiny watch screw when she went back downstairs. To avoid any suspicion from Pelina, he called Oza up one day to help him find a screw. Some of those screws in watches are so tiny it's almost impossible to find them. Hollis was always very careful never to drop a screw on the floor. If he dropped a screw, it always landed on his work table. Oza looked and looked but could never find the screw because, of course, there was never a screw on the floor to begin with. Hollis cursed and kicked Oza and yelled at him to go back downstairs. From then on it was always Dorothy who could find the screws he supposedly dropped.

There was no water at the Marsh homestead and Dorothy and the older children had to carry buckets of water from the well at the place from which they had moved. Pelina's brother, Willie, offered to help Hollis dig a well.

During the day, Hollis and Willie had taken turns pulling themselves out of the well by using a rope tied to a small tree. Then, taking the rope from their waist, they would tie it to the handle of a five-gallon can and lower it into the well. The one in the well would fill the can with dirt for the one outside to pull out. Once the dirt was out, he would lower himself back down to help dig. Suddenly, they struck water. It came gushing out and within minutes had the bottom of the well covered. Quickly, they looked up and saw the rope was out of their reach. Without thinking, they had dug themselves deeper than the rope was long. They called to Pelina for help. Looking into the well, she saw the desperate situation they were in.

She became too frightened to think about her unborn baby. Quickly, she untied the rope from the tree and lowered it down enough for the men to reach. Willie quickly tied the rope around Hollis' waist since he was the smaller of the two. Struggling with all her might, Pelina pulled her husband to the top. Then she and Hollis hauled her brother out of the deep hole.

That night her child was born.

Spring arrived and Pelina could hardly wait to see fresh vegetables growing in her garden. However, her garden was mostly filled with tree stumps and roots. Hollis was given an old plow that a neighbor no longer used. He tied both ends of a rope to the plow. He told Dorothy and Oza to step inside of the circled rope and hold it up around their waists. He ordered Pelina to hold the plow straight in the ground. It was in this manner that the garden was plowed the first year at their new home.

The dishes that Pelina's mother had given her when she got married were now long gone, broken by small hands. Pelina had a collection of lids from one-gallon tin lard buckets that the family used as plates. For drinking, they used tin cans with the sharp edges rolled under until they were smooth enough to drink from. The Marsh children did not receive toys at Christmas and they had very few playthings. Yet Hollis possessed another unique talent, former neighbors said. He could make toys. He made the only wagon the children ever had and he also, through the years, made mechanical toys carved from wood.

During the middle of the 1940s, Pelina heard that one of the nurseries was hiring workers to sucker the young trees. The job was paying seventy-five cents a day. Pelina was pregnant, but she wanted a job to provide the basic necessities for her children.

Hollis was jealous of Pelina and did not want her going anywhere without him. So she asked her brother, Jack, to get a job at the nursery too so she could go to work with him. "Me and Pelina both went to work at the nursery," Jack said. "But Hollis, he wouldn't go to work for anybody," said Jack, now a McMinnville businessman. "A lot of people offered him a job as a mechanic because he was so good, but he wouldn't take it. But he did like to play the fiddle. He could play just about any kind of musical instrument, guitar, fiddle, mandolin — but the fiddle was his favorite," said Jack.

Dorothy stayed home taking care of the younger children. In the mornings, she helped her mother fix a breakfast of biscuits, sometimes with water and without shortening. The biscuits were supplemented with water gravy and unsweetened blackberries. The children hardly ever saw any milk in their house.

Dorothy usually cooked the other meals for the family. These consisted mainly of peas or beans served up with cornbread made with water. One day an aunt was there when Dorothy was making cornbread for supper. She was stirring it in a big pan with her hand. "Dorothy, you don't stir cornbread with your hand, you need a big spoon," the aunt said. "By Ned," Dorothy replied, "there's so much of this stuff I have to stir it with my hand!"

Pelina was desperate to feed her growing family without calling on her aging parents for help. She confided to a younger sister that it was her prayer that before she died she would see the day when she would have all the food she wanted to eat.

In the summers during the blackberry season, Hollis would drive Pelina and the children back to her parents. They would spend about three weeks helping the rest of the family pick berries and can them. The family would take home dozens of cans filled with blackberry jam, jelly, and canned berries to be made into pies later, or simply eaten in a bowl with sugar over them.

With the Marsh family increasing so rapidly, it was only a matter of years until their two-seated A-Model Ford was too small for them. That was the only car they ever owned, but in those days cars were built to last longer and Hollis was a good mechanic. After a number of years, that old car rattled, groaned and moaned, but it never stopped running.

Hollis quickly solved the problem of overcrowding when traveling with his family. He built a flatbed trailer with sides about one foot high, and hitched it to the back of the old A-Model. Only the older children were allowed to ride in it with strict orders to never stand up nor to move about.

One hot summer day, they were headed down to DeKalb County for blackberry picking. The old car made so much noise, it could be heard from miles away.

Out on her back porch, Margaret heard the car about a mile away, chugging and spurting slowly down the road. Then suddenly, all was quiet, and Margaret knew something had happened. While they were traveling down a hill, the trailer had broken loose from the car. Dorothy and the other children in the trailer panicked; their screams, however, went unheard. Immediately, the trailer swerved off of the road and into a ditch landing upside down.

Hollis drove on, not knowing that anything had happened. When he started up the next hill, he realized the car was pulling the trailer much easier than usual. Stretching his neck out of the window, he saw that the trailer was missing.

"Where in the hell is that trailer?" he shouted, panic-stricken, as he swerved the car around and headed back up the road.

A short distance away, they saw the children climbing out of the ditch. Luckily they had gone through that ordeal without a scratch.

Later that day. Dorothy told an aunt that she would never have more children than could be seated in the car with her.

Listen to the Sound

The Marshes lived across the field from the W.E. Morgan family. The Morgans raised vegetables for the Kroger and H.G. Hill grocery chains. Pelina and Dorothy worked in the fields for the Morgans, harvesting crowder peas, black-eyed peas, and bell peppers. Instead of cash, they often were paid with vegetables that were not up to market standards. Hollis and Pelina never had enough money to buy a pig or a cow so they could have something of their own to feed their family.

Most of Dorothy's clothes in those years were hand-me-downs from Addie Morgan, now Addie Glenn, still a resident of the Moore's College Community. "I knew Dorothy all my life," said Addie. "I was about two years older than her and we used to run around together." Dorothy also went with the Morgans to the Bluff Springs Church of Christ.

The Morgans took Dorothy to see her first movie when she was about twelve years old.

"Daddy used to take his truck all around the community on Saturday mornings, picking up people who wanted to go into McMinnville to buy their groceries or to go to the movies," Addie said. "One Saturday, Dorothy went on the truck with us and some of us kids went to the movies. It was one of those westerns with a lot of fighting and shooting and Dorothy was frightened." The little country girl who was frightened by the first movie she ever saw, later would herself act in movies and on stage in addition to becoming one of the best-known country music artists of her time.

"Dorothy didn't get a chance to ride in a car very often so when she went somewhere with us, she always wanted to sit in the front seat and we let her," relates Addie. "I always felt sorry for Dorothy because she really had a hard row to hoe."

Addie said the Marsh family survived because Pelina was a survivor. She took the clothes that neighbors and relatives gave the family, mended them, and altered them to fit her brood. She was able to keep her family clean and dressed as well as many of the other children in that rural area of the South.

"When she was pregnant and would keep coming to work in the fields, my daddy would say 'Pelina, you ought not to be working like this' and she would say, 'It won't hurt me none,' and would just keep working.

"Dorothy had a lot of Pelina in her to keep going the way she did through all the things the girl faced in her lifetime," Addie said.

Youngsters in the Moore's College Community played baseball every Saturday afternoon in someone's yard, often at the Marshes's house. Years later, the Dottie West Ballpark in McMinnville, named for the country star, would offer recreational facilities for countless numbers of local people of all ages.

In the summertime on Friday and Saturday nights, there was much enjoyment at the Marsh house. The young uncles, aunts, cousins, and neighboring young people gathered in their yard to sing by the moonlight. There was not enough room in the little cabin to get that many people inside. Hollis played the fiddle and Pelina was the lead singer.

Some would walk for miles across the

fields and through the woods to get to the
cabin.

"You could hear the music a half-mile
away," said one neighbor.

"Hollis always enjoyed these get-togethers
and he was always nice to us," said Willie.
"That's one reason we never knew how bad
things really were for Pelina and the children."

Some of the young boys and girls got together and came as dates. Pretty soon, news
traveled throughout the community that this
was a good place to carry your date. Everyone could have a good time without spending
money. But it was different with Dorothy.
She was not allowed to date anyone. One
Saturday night, Hollis caught her looking at
Norman Gene Hutchins, a young neighbor
boy she admired a lot, yet no one knew it. After everyone had gone, Dorothy got the beat-
ing of her life. She carried welts and bruises
for weeks. Never again did Dorothy ever look
at another boy in the presence of Hollis.

In the wintertime, the Marshes always listened to the Grand Ole Opry. "It wasn't everybody out there in the country in those

days who had a radio," remembers brother Jack. "But Hollis had an old battered radio and that's why they always had a radio to listen to. Hollis knew how to keep the battery charged."

Jack remembers when comedienne Minnie Pearl went on the Grand Ole Opry in October, 1940. The gracious Southern lady from Centerville, Tennessee, whose ambition had been to become a dramatic actress, soon was a hit with country radio listeners and later was a popular performer on television. In 1974, she was inducted into the Country Music Hall of Fame in Nashville, an unprecedented tribute for a performer who was neither a singer nor a musician.

The avid Grand Ole Opry fans who gathered at the Marsh cabin every Saturday night were soon imitating Minnie Pearl's shrill "How-DEE!" as they already would gleefully mimic the Solemn Ole Judge's line, "Let 'er go, boys!" that opened every session of the Grand Ole Opry.

There were not yet any women singers on the country music show from Nashville, but already some of the female singers who would become legends on the Grand Ole Opry were coming into the rural homes of the South over other radio stations. In those years before television, radio was king.

The Carter Family group of Alvin Carter, his wife, Sara, and his sister-in-law, Maybelle Carter, had made recordings of "Wildwood Flower" and "Keep on the Sunny Side," both of which had become well-known throughout the South. In 1938, the Carters began singing on the 50,000-watt Mexican border station of XERA in Del Rio, Texas. By 1943, Maybelle Carter and her daughters, Helen, June, and Anita, were performing to audiences around the country as Mother Maybelle and the Carter Sisters.

Twelve-year-old Dorothy's greatest longing now was not for food, which was scarce in their house, nor for greater creature comforts in the rough cabin where the Marsh family lived — but for a guitar.

Then came what seemed to her a miraculous development. Her school was going to sell Rosebud Salve as a fund-raising effort, and the student who sold the most boxes of salve would receive a prize — a guitar.

Every day after school and on weekends, Dorothy walked for miles through the hollows and up and down the hills, selling the sweet-smelling ointment. She was the top salesperson in the school, and then she began the agonizing wait for the coveted instrument to arrive in the mail.

But when the day finally came, the young girl was sick in bed with the measles. Although feverish and uncomfortable, she sat up in bed long enough to take the precious guitar from its box and then lie back lightly strumming the instrument. That night, she fell asleep with her thin arms wrapped around her prize. "Dorothy loved that guitar," Addie Glenn recalls. "She would just pick and sing and say 'One of these days, I'm going to be on the Grand Ole Opry.'" That seemed an unlikely goal for a girl from a poverty-stricken family in rural Tennessee in the early 1940s.

Pelina was excited about the new job she had as a cook in the lunchroom at Moore's College Elementary School, which her children attended. Not even the deep cold of a harsh winter would stand in her way.

With her working regularly, things were looking up for the Marsh family. Every morning, Pelina would bundle up the youngest children, put them in the homemade wagon, and pull them to a neighbor, who would look after them while she and the older children were at school. A few weeks after starting her job she made a suggestion that was accepted by the principal, and that the teachers also thought would be a good thing to do—Pelina would have a snack ready for the children at their recess time. They could pass through the lunchroom and get it on their way out to play. Pelina wanted to keep her children and others in similar economic circumstances from being hungry.

During the school term, the Marsh children got their best meal of the day at school. Also, the meals were free for children of underprivileged families like them.

Farther back through the woods and near a creek, a four-bedroom house with five acres of land went up for sale about one mile from the Marsh cabin. The house had a large kitchen and dining room, something Pelina had been dreaming of having for her own. She realized that with her children they had long outgrown the cabin. In fact, they had outgrown that cabin before they moved in. Hollis and Pelina let their little cabin be the down payment on the larger house, plus they would still have payments of $20.00 a month. Along with the house came a mule and a barn full of hay. The Marshes looked forward to spring when they could plant a large garden and the remaining acres in corn.

Dorothy at last had a bedroom to herself,

but, she had to fill the cracks between the log walls with rags and newspapers. The wind whipped through the room with such velocity it would blow out the lamplight at night when she was trying to study. Sometimes while she was asleep the wind would blow the stuffing out and the snow would cover her bed. In spite of that, she was still proud of her bedroom.

On a cold morning before dawn in March of 1948, when Dorothy was fifteen, Pelina had a miscarriage. Hollis woke Dorothy up and told her to find the baby in the bloody discharge in her mother's bed. The girl found the body of the baby boy and wrapped it in a newspaper, the only material she could find.

Terrified that her mother was dying, but equally terrified of defying Hollis' orders, Dorothy, with tears streaming down her cheeks, dug a hole near the kitchen window and buried the tiny baby. She carried out her gruesome task by the light of the moon.

Later that day, Pelina was taken to the hospital in McMinnville in critical condition.

Pelina stayed in the hospital for two months before she was strong enough to undergo a hysterectomy. After her surgery, her doctor sent her to one of her sister's homes to recuperate instead of to her own home, where the heavy responsibilities of a family of ten children would rest once again upon her frail shoulders.

Bill and Margaret were not able to give the help to Pelina's family they once had given. Bill was now nearly eighty years old and, in addition, Grandmother Walker, Margaret's aged mother, had moved in with them.

Hollis warned the children not to tell Pelina's relatives what a hard time they were having. At one point, the only food they had for three days was blackberries they would go out and pick each day. Hollis continued to molest Dorothy.

One afternoon Hollis became irritated when Dorothy and her sister were arguing over who was to wash the dishes and who was to dry them. Hollis jerked his belt off to whip Dorothy. She ran out of the house and down the hill to the creek, hoping he would not come after her. Too late, she realized she had done the wrong thing. As Hollis went down the steps, he dropped his belt on the porch. He took his knife from his pocket and in the edge of the woods he cut a limb from a large sapling with the razor-sharp blade. "If you run another step from me, you will never live to climb this hill again," he hollered at her. Dorothy stopped, she was so frightened, her whole body shook. "Daddy, please don't, I'm sorry. I will always dry the dishes from now on. Please don't whip me," she cried. By then, Hollis was down to where Dorothy was standing by the water. With the long limb, he drew back and it came down hard on her, knocking her into the water. Cursing about every breath, he ordered her up. Quickly, Dorothy got up and tried to run back up the hill, but Hollis was right behind her. Again she fell but this time she was not able to plead for her life. At this point, Hollis realized he had beaten Dorothy too severly. He helped her up the hill and into the house. A few hours later, Hollis sent for a neighbor to help get Dorothy to the hospital.

Dorothy was too hysterical to talk to the doctor. She kept repeating, "cause . . . cause . . . cause."

The doctor gave her a shot to calm her down and to make her sleep the rest of the night. But he then sent the child back home with her daddy.

Later that night, Dorothy was awakened by stomach cramps. She tossed and turned. Finally, she went out on the side porch next to her bedroom. As the pains worsened, she thought walking might help. She went down to the creek to keep out of view of her daddy, just in case he awoke and looked out of the window. Suddenly, she felt a gush come from her body, and she knew she had had a miscarriage. A few days before then, she had begun to suspect that she might be pregnant by her daddy. Near daybreak, she slowly made her way back up the hill and into bed.

When noon came and Dorothy had not gotten up, Hollis went to her door and stormed, "Get out of that bed now."

Dorothy felt too weak to walk, but she knew better than to lie in bed.

Dorothy went out into the yard where the other children were. She felt more protected from her daddy when she was around them.

Dorothy fainted and fell hard on the ground. The other children began screaming. Hollis ran out to see what the commotion was. He grabbed a gallon bucket and soused it into the rainbarrel and poured the full gallon of water on Dorothy's face to revive her.

"You damn little tramp, if that's how you're going to act, get back in bed."

S E V E N

Justice

The summer had passed by without any soil being tilled. Not one seed had Hollis put in the ground. There would be no garden or fields of corn that year.

The little barn had long been empty of hay. The protruding ribs of the mule proved how little nourishment he was getting from the dried-up pastureland.

Hollis did not keep up the payments on the farm, and by the time Pelina was able to return home, they were facing foreclosure. Hollis found a four-room house for rent in the community of Green's Cross Roads. The family of twelve moved into the shack back in the woods. There was scarcely any room for them to walk around inside the house. But there were darker forces at work within the family that Pelina would know nothing of for a long time.

Pelina's daddy died in the spring of 1949. Neighbors and friends throughout the area filled his yard and large farmhouse for two days and nights, bringing food and paying their respects to the highly respected farmer and community leader. He was buried in the cemetery of New Union Baptist Church, for which he had given the land.

After his first wife's death, he had erected an iron fence around an area that would be the Jones' plot. Today, two tombstones stand at his grave along with his wives — with his and Louisa's name on one, and his and Margaret's name on the other one.

Hollis' meanness and drunkenness continued to hold the family in fear and shame. Pelina and the children never knew from one day to the next what he would do. One day, he ordered Pelina and Dorothy out of the house with a gun. He made them sit down on a tree stump and held the gun to them, threatening to kill them. At that moment, a man named Buck Chisiam arrived and saw what was happening. He took the gun from

Hollis and carried it home with him. Later he paid Hollis for the gun to keep from bringing it back.

That fall Dorothy and her brother, Oza, were riding the school bus to Central High School in McMinnville. The other children, who were old enough to go to school, were attending a school close to Green's Cross Roads.

She was a junior that year, when on October 11, her seventeenth birthday, Hollis told her to bring all of her books home from school that day because she was not going back. She was now past the age of compulsory school attendance required by Tennessee law. "You will never go to school again," he told her. "From now on, you will stay at home and do the work here."

The young girl had never been allowed to have much of a social life outside of her family, and she had never had a date. Now she was being condemned to spend her life in a shack in the woods taking care of her younger brothers and sisters. This, at least, was what Hollis wanted Dorothy and Pelina to think. Pelina felt she had no choice but to speak up. Her greatest dream was to see all of her children graduate from high school.

"Hollis, you can't mean that. Dorothy only has two years left. Please let her stay in school." Before Pelina could scarely get those last words from her mouth, a tin plate bounced off the side of her head.

"You keep your damn trap shut, I don't need you poking your nose in my business," he stormed out at her. Pelina turned and left the room, feeling dizzy from the hard blow to her head.

A few weeks before then, Hollis had met one of his neighbors in town who worked in Detroit, Michigan, for Ford Motor Company. Hollis asked him about the work at Ford. "There's still openings and the pay is good. You should go up and get you a job," the neighbor informed him.

"That's what I've been thinking of doing. I'm taking Dorothy out of school and she's going with me and keep house and cook for me," answered Hollis. But Hollis had not mentioned to Pelina or Dorothy what his plans were.

Stunned and confused, Dorothy rode the school bus into town that day and took her regular seat in the classroom. As the full implication of what her daddy was going to force her to do sank in, she began to suddenly sob uncontrollably. The teacher rushed to her side, but the girl was unable to tell her what was wrong.

In the principal's office though, Dorothy

broke down and in a flood of tears revealed what she had been subjected to at home for years. The principal immediately called Warren County Sheriff R.S. Cantrell. Cantrell knew the Marsh family because his wife, Harriet, was a sister to Kermit Turner, Pelina's brother-in-law.

Cantrell called Harriet from the school and told her that Dorothy Marsh would be staying with them for a few days. He told Dorothy he was going to lock her daddy up and see that he never hurt her or anyone else again.

In a short time, Cantrell and two of his deputies were on the road to Green's Cross Roads. Pelina had just stepped out of the house into the yard when she saw the sheriff's car coming down the road.

"Pelina, where is Hollis?" Cantrell asked as soon as he got out of his car. That question brought Hollis from the car that he was working on in the front yard, but, before he could say anything, handcuffs were slapped on his wrists by the two deputies.

"What have I done?" Hollis demanded of the sheriff. "Why are you arresting me?"

"You'll find out," snapped the sheriff.

The sheriff left without explaining anything to Pelina, but later that afternoon, Cantrell returned to explain to a disbelieving

Pelina the charges that had been lodged against her husband—rape, incest, and violating the age of consent law. His bond had been set at $35,000. Cantrell assured Pelina that Dorothy was safe at his house in Mc-Minnville.

Meanwhile, Jack, who was helping Hollis work on the car when Hollis was arrested, stayed with Pelina and the other children.

Harriet knew it was Dorothy's birthday and she surprised the scared, unhappy and very underweight girl. At dinner that night she was presented with the first birthday cake she had ever had, complete with ice cream. When dinner was over, Harriet took Dorothy to town to one of the stores that was still open and bought her the prettiest "store-bought" clothes that she had ever worn.

For the next few nights, Dorothy was too frightened to sleep very much. She kept thinking her daddy would break out of jail and go back and kill her mother. Pelina was also scared. What little sleep she got was sitting in a rocker near the front door in case Hollis broke out and came back.

On the second night, Pelina dropped off to sleep. Suddenly a noise on the front porch woke her. She began trembling, and her legs became so weak she could hardly walk. She woke up Jack. "Get up quick, I believe Hollis is here," she whispered. Jack rushed to the front window but there was no one outside. Quickly, he opened the door. A large 'possum ran off the porch. He closed the door, assuring Pelina that all was safe.

Three days later, Dorothy returned home to Green's Cross Roads. Jack was still staying at Pelina's house.

The next week, Pelina took the children and moved into an apartment, owned by her cousin, McMinnville Mayor Vernon Jones. Penniless and with ten children dependent upon her, she went on public welfare. The apartment had only three rooms, but Pelina didn't mind as long as they were safe from Hollis. Now Dorothy and Oza could walk the five blocks home each day for lunch.

The following January, a circuit court jury brought a verdict of guilty on all three charges against Hollis and he was sentenced to forty years in the Tennessee State Penitentiary. The sentence was imposed on Friday afternoon and Hollis was transported to Nashville on Monday.

Bill and Margaret Jones
Dottie's grandparents
(Pelina's mother and father)

Dottie's birthplace in
Smithville, TN.

Dottie, age 4, with mother Pelina and
three of her siblings.

The window of Dottie's bedroom in the attic can be seen in this photo of the house where 12 people lived.

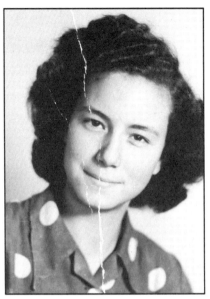

Dottie age 12

The Marsh family in 1946. Dottie is second from left in the back row.

Dottie at age 17
with her great
grandmother
Pelina Walker

Dottie and Kathy Dee performed on the
Landmark Jamboree as the Kay-Dots.

Marsh Sentenced To 40-Year Prison Term

A Circuit Court jury brought back a verdict of guilty on a statutory charge against a Warren farmer-mechanic last Friday and sentenced the convicted man to not more than 40 years in the state penitentiary.

Committed to the penal institution Monday afternoon was Hollis Marsh, a resident of the north part of Warren county who was charged in a Grand Jury indictment with rape upon the person of a member of his household.

A crowded courtroom witnessed the day-long proceedings and heard the testimony of a number of witnesses mount the evidence against the accused man. The defendant took the stand in his own behalf late in the proceedings.

Asst. Atty. Gen. Robert S. Brady, prosecuting the case for the state, asked the jury for conviction on the capitol charge and after the case was closed the jury deliberated less than an hour before returning the guilty verdict.

Morford W. Locke, appointed by the court to represent the defendant, indicated last Saturday that he would not seek a new trial and that no motion, on his part, would be entered in the case.

Sheriff R. S. Cantrell stated that state prison authorities came for the convicted man Monday and he was returned to the Nashville confinement that afternoon

STANDARD PRINTING CO.
McMinnville, Tennessee

One of Dottie's first
publicity photos.

Dottie appeared frequently
on the Grand Ole Opry
in the early 1960s.

—*photo by Hope Powell*

Dottie's mother, Pelina

Dottie formed the Heartaches with husband Bill West (back row, center)

Dottie greets fans following a concert

Dottie liked flashy clothes.
Notice the rhinestones
on this bluejean outfit.
—*photo by Hope Powell*

Dottie in 1977

Dottie with Dolly Parton
and Larry Gatlin.
—*photo by Hope Powell*

Dottie in the 80s

Dottie with third husband
Alan Carter Winters
—*photo by Hope Powell*

Dottie—fifty and feisty
—*photo by Hope Powell*

Dottie's gravesite in McMinnville, Tennessee

E I G H T

Let Freedom Sing

For the first time in her life, things were looking up for Dorothy and the rest of the Marsh family. Dorothy, who was now called Dottie, was free to have friends and a social life. She became a guitar player and singer in a high school band called The Coonskins, formed by some third-year high school boys as a Future Farmers of America project.

The Coonskins were led by Joe Kuhn, who played the fiddle. Other band members were Joe Bob Basham, Don Blankenship, Charles Webster, and Wayne York.

"I played the guitar and did the singing even though I really can't sing a lick," Joe Bob, now a correctional officer with the Warren County Sheriff's Department, remembers. "Then Dottie joined us. It was clear that she had the singing talent and I didn't, so she was our singer," he said.

The youngsters, dressed in Western outfits, soon were a popular attraction in the area, playing not only at their high school assemblies but for square dances at the local VFW club and company picnics. They eventually persuaded McMinnville's WMMT radio station owners, Hal and Aaron Durham, to broadcast the group's music. The paths of Dottie Marsh and Hal Durham would cross again in Nashville years later, when Hal Durham became manager of the Grand Ole Opry, and Dottie was one of its brightest stars.

"When we had our band, I was playing a Silvertone guitar from Sears Roebuck," Joe Bob recalled. "Dottie used to like to borrow it because it was better than hers."

Joe Bob also had an old car that the band used to get to their engagements.

"Dottie used to ask me to take her to Nashville to the Grand Ole Opry," said Basham. "But I was afraid we would get off up there and the car would break down so I never took her."

"But I've always regretted that I didn't," he added.

Pelina's first job after Hollis' sentence was at the McMinnville Garment Factory. Even though it would only be a temporary job, it was a beginning for her. Making men's pants was hard work, but she had no trouble reaching production every day that she was there. Since she knew the job was for only a short time, she did not report it to the welfare office. After all, she was barely receiving enough from the welfare department to make ends meet.

The three months that Pelina worked was enough time to give her a taste of what it was like to work in public. She liked her job, and she loved the people. For eighteen years she had been kept in the backwoods with no one to talk to but her children. Now life for her was like stepping into a whole new world.

The next morning she was up and waiting for Jack Smartt's restaurant to open. She had been told that they needed someone to work. When she applied for the job, they gave her an apron and put her to work. She liked the restaurant work much more than the garment job, mostly because she met people. She loved everybody, and never met a stranger. More and more people began coming back, and it's been said that it was because of the love and attention Pelina gave them.

When school was out, Dottie got a job at

the same restaurant, but she was not as en-
thusiastic about her job as Pelina was. During her first week on the job, she was carrying a tray of food, coffee and tea over her
shoulder and balanced on one hand. Dottie
was feeling proud of herself until she
stepped in spilled water. Her feet flew out
from under her and down she went. The
customers sitting near Dottie, surprisingly
got food and drinks they did not order,
served to them on their clothes. Dottie was
more careful from then on.

Meanwhile, Pelina had been saving money to rent a house. She had kept her children cramped up for too long in the three-
room apartment. They needed a yard, a
place where they could run and play. Pelina
found a four-bedroom frame house on An-
derson Street.

The welfare workers visited her and told
her she could not work and continue to receive welfare benefits. Her answer was to get
a second job and get off of public welfare.
For another year Pelina worked two jobs and
saved all she could.

When Bond's Funeral Home went out of
business, Pelina knew that it would be a
good place for a restaurant. It was located
across the street from the square.

Pelina, who had a reputation as a good

cook, even though she never had much food to cook, would soon open her own restaurant — and later, even a second one. For the first time in her life, she would be able to cook as much food, and as many kinds, as she wanted to, for herself, her family, and her customers. She also would be able to raise and educate her children.

Pelina was so grateful for her own good fortune that she wanted to share with others. When families were at the funeral home near her restaurant holding a wake for a loved one, she sent over enough food to provide for all the bereaved without charge, even though some were strangers to her.

NINE

Lift Up Thy Voice

With the help of McMinnville businessmen, Dottie got a scholarship to attend Tennessee Polytechnic Institute, now Tennessee Technological University, or Tennessee Tech, in nearby Cookeville. She would major in music.

On her first night on campus, she sang in the college's traditional "first-night" talent show. That night she met Bill West, a soft-spoken steel guitar player from Nashville, who was working toward a degree in electrical engineering. In the freshman talent segment, somebody asked Bill to play his guitar while Dottie sang. Country music history was made that night. There would come a time when their Heartaches Band would perform in auditoriums and coliseums across the United States and in Europe, and

Dottie would rack up some of the most prestigious singing awards in the business.

Soon after they met, Dottie and Bill formed a country music band that played at dances, dinners and other social functions in and around Cookeville. As a pun on their college's well-known "Tech Troubadours" dance band, they called their group the "Tech Two By Fours."

Friends knew how proud Dottie was of her white cowgirl boots she wore when she and Bill and the band had an engagement. She always wore the boots to school on the day the band was going to sing that night.

She was also working in the B&B Restaurant in Cookeville to help pay her way through school.

By their sophomore year, Dottie and Bill, now married, were pictured in the 1953 *Eagle*, the Tech year book, in headshots side by side as "Dot West" and "Bill West." They moved into the veterans' housing—prefabricated buildings brought from a government shipyard on the Gulf Coast and set up on the campus to accommodate the World War II veterans who flooded college campuses after the war, getting their education on the G.I. Bill.

At Tennessee Tech were many young men from surrounding counties that had been listed in federal government statistics as some of the poorest counties in the nation. Just out of military service, the veterans came to get a college education in Cookeville. They came wearing their old army khaki, a move that trashed any collegiate dress code the school might have had. Many of the veterans came with wives and children in tow. By 1953, however, the veteran enrollment had reached its peak and the former veterans' housing was opened to non-veteran married students as it became available.

Sons, Morris and Kerry, the first two of Dottie and Bill's four children, were born while the couple was still in college. After Bill's graduation, they moved to Cleveland, Ohio, where Bill got a job as an electrical engineer.

Dottie began selling Stanley products to help out with the finances. However, she was determined to sing. She landed a job on the *Landmark Jamboree*, a Cleveland country and western television show. It was on this show that she met songstress Kathy Dee from West Virginia. They sang together as

The Kay-Dots. Here, she also met several Grand Ole Opry singers from Nashville who came up to Cleveland to guest star on the *Landmark Jamboree*.

It was in Cleveland that Bill and Dot's daughter, Shelly, was born, named for Dot's favorite movie actress, Shelley Winters.

After nearly five years on the Cleveland show, Dottie learned it was going to be dropped. Dottie and Bill came to Nashville on vacation and spent the days making the rounds of recording studios without success. They were on their way back to Cleveland, disappointed and defeated, when heading out of Nashville on Dickerson Road, they saw the new studio of Starday Music Company.

"I asked Bill if he would just sit in the car with the kids while I went in and tried one more time to get somebody to give me a chance," Dottie recalled to a newspaper reporter friend.

She talked with Don Pierce in the studio. One week later, she was back in Nashville to cut "Angel on Paper" for Starday. It cost her $511 to cut the record. On the recording, she changed her name to Dottie. Nashville disc jockeys played it over local stations and Ott Devine, manager of the Grand Ole Opry, heard it and asked her to be a guest on the

Saturday night show that performed on the stage of the Ryman Auditorium in downtown Nashville. "That was when my dream was fulfilled," Dottie said, "that first time I appeared on the Grand Ole Opry."

But at first, Dottie made guest appearances on the Opry only about once every two or three months for about a year, she and Bill and the three children driving in an old model car to Nashville from Cleveland. Then with the $1,000 they had saved, Bill gave up his job in Cleveland and they came back to Nashville to take their chances on making it in country music. They moved in with Bill's parents in West Nashville, but only until they could find a house.

Dottie and Bill wanted a house near Mrs. West so she could help them with the children. A week later, a short distance from Mrs. West, they found a three-bedroom pink cottage. The color pleased Dottie. "Our convertible is white, our house is pink and I want a pink kitchen," she told a friend. Things were looking up. Dottie had no intentions of ever looking back.

Dottie was still following her star.

With only one record and a scrapbook of newspaper clippings about what she had done in Cleveland, Dottie went to Lucky Moeller, manager of the largest booking agency in the world for country music. Lucky signed her.

That following summer she got the opportunity to be in a movie with Sonny James. The movie was to be made in Florida. With excitement, she and Bill loaded up the children and off they went. Dottie worked hard, but on the last day of filming she was told that the producers had run out of money and the movie could not be finished. Dottie was disappointed for a few days, but, realizing that singing was her dream, she snapped out of her depression. "Aw shucks, I still have my life ahead of me. I can make my dreams come true," she said.

The young girl of Warren County that just a short time ago felt her life was doomed told an aunt, "There were so many times I felt like giving up but yet, there was a force within me that kept nudging me on."

As Dottie spoke, she smiled as she held in her hands a *Billboard* magazine showing that her latest recording had reached number one.

Dottie was feeling the realization of her dreams. However, her greatest moments were on the stage of the Grand Ole Opry.

On January 21, 1962, Dottie gave birth to their fourth child, Dale.

By now, they were financially able to hire

a full-time babysitter, Jean McDaniel. She immediately fell in love with the children. Bill's mother had been graciously kind to keep the children before then while Bill's father stayed at home and took care of the farm. However, each day he always drove down to Bill's house to make sure his wife and the children were okay and to see if they needed anything from the store. But as time went by, his health began to fail and Bill's mother needed to be at home more.

One morning when Dottie, Jean and the children were home alone, Dottie had the scare of her life. Dottie was talking on the phone, near the kitchen window when suddenly the phone went dead. About then, Dottie saw a man in prison clothes going around her house. She didn't get a good look at his face but she just knew it was her daddy coming back to kill her. The state prison where he was, was only a few miles away. Dottie and Jean quickly checked all of the doors and windows to be sure they were locked. Rushing into the kitchen with the children, they leaned the backs of chairs under the doorknobs for extra protection.

Hurrying back to the windows, Dottie pulled the shades down to keep him from looking in. Again and again, Dottie tried to call the police, but her phone was completely dead. She realized her phone line had been cut. At one point, the front door shook hard. They expected him to break it down at any time. Then finally, everything became quiet. Dottie peeked out of the front kitchen window and didn't see him. She crossed the room and peeked out of the back window and saw him sitting in a chair under a shade tree. "Thank God," she whispered, "It's not Daddy." Jean was holding the baby to keep him quiet.

In the meantime, Mrs. West had been trying to call Dottie. Finally, she decided to go over there. Dottie met her at the door and gave her the news. She rushed back home and called the police. Then Mr. and Mrs. West went back to Dottie's house not knowing how things would be. However, Mrs. West's car had frightened the criminal from the backyard into some tall weeds. The police found the fugitive a short distance away on the banks of the Cumberland River.

After that, Dottie never enjoyed living there. She was never at ease, knowing she was just a few miles from her daddy. Within a year, Hollis did make headlines. He killed a man.

Bill and Dottie were traveling a lot but she worried about Jean and the children while they were away. "But I would never do a show without Bill on stage with me," she said. All of Dottie's relatives adored Bill. Not once had they ever seen him upset or angry with Dottie. He had a great personality and a deep love for all mankind.

TEN

Rainbows

Dottie soon became close friends with a singer who had been on the show only three years earlier — Patsy Cline.

Cline, a native of Virginia, made country music history with such Top 10 records as "I Fall to Pieces" in 1961, "Crazy" in 1962 and "Sweet Dreams," recorded exactly one month before she was killed in a plane crash on March 5, 1963 at the age of thirty, at the pinnacle of her career.

Patsy, who was exactly thirty-four days older than Dottie, often invited Dottie to sit in on her recording sessions with Owen Bradley, a producer whose credits included records by some of the greatest stars to come out of Nashville, including Kitty Wells, Ernest Tubb, and Red Foley.

Patsy Cline was one of the first women to

headline a show, making her the closing act or main attraction rather than being the opening act for a man. In 1962, she was one of the first country acts to headline in Las Vegas. Dottie West later would play the glitzy city.

In those years, most of the Grand Ole Opry artists were keeping up a grueling schedule of two or three weeks on the road playing one-night stands and making it back to Nashville for at least twenty-six weekends a year. They usually traveled in a luxury Cadillac, often carrying as many as five people and some instruments, but which was comfortable and roomy enough for sleeping as they traveled from one city to another across the nation. Some eventually bought buses to transport their band members and instruments to their engagements.

In recalling some of her most frightening road experiences, Dottie once told of her, Bill and a couple of band members becoming marooned in a blizzard on a highway in the Midwest. They knew they were hitting bad weather but they were pushed for time and decided to continue driving in the snow. "But it became so thick we couldn't see where we were going and we couldn't even tell if we were still on the highway," she recalled. They were stuck in snow drifts in sub-zero temperatures and thought they would surely freeze to death before they were found. They kept the car radio on to get reports of the storm and of rescue operations.

"Then we heard our song, 'Paper Mansions' and we thought that might ease our going out—listening to our first hit song as we froze to death," she said. Hours later, they were found and snow plows pulled them out of their snowbound tomb.

Meanwhile, the Opry comedienne Minnie Pearl, whose real name is Ophelia Colley, had married Henry Cannon, a former Air Corps pilot who now was a partner in a charter flying service. Promoters started using Cannon's DC-3s to take package shows of six or seven acts to the West Coast, where country music had not yet attracted a lot of attention.

But because Minnie Pearl and her husband were often on engagements in different parts of the country, Henry Cannon sold his partner his half-interest in the charter service. Cannon kept a Beechcraft plane, which he used in a private charter service for Opry stars. Now he was flying Minnie to all of her performances.

Those were the days of two-lane highways, before the advent of the interstate highway system that enabled people to move quickly across the country in their cars. Many of the Opry entertainers decided the small private airplane were the way to go.

One of those who moved with the trend was Randy Hughes, Patsy Cline's manager and son-in-law of Opry entertainer, Lloyd "Cowboy" Copas.

On March 3, 1963, Hughes brought Patsy and her husband, Charlie Dick, into Nashville from an engagement in Birmingham, Alabama. Because of her busy schedule, Patsy was a last-minute addition to a performance with a group of country artists, including Dottie and Bill West, who were putting on a concert in Kansas City, Missouri for the family of a Kansas City disc jockey who had been killed in an automobile accident.

Patsy's husband got off at the small private airport in Nashville while Patsy and Randy gassed up the plane and took off for Kansas City. "Patsy closed the show that night and she was the star of the show," said Dottie West "She was wearing a white chiffon dress and I said, 'My God, she sings like an angel and she looks like one'."

March 4, 1963, dawned foggy and rainy in Kansas City. Randy Hughes kept calling the weather bureau but could not get clearance for flying. Dottie invited Patsy to ride back to Nashville in the car with her and Bill, and Patsy almost accepted the offer. But on March 5, Randy decided to head the plane to Nashville. Flying back with Patsy and Randy were fellow country stars, Cowboy Copas and Hawkshaw Hawkins.

The last words Dottie said to her friend were, "Patsy, I'm really going to be worried about you flying in this weather," to which Patsy replied, "Don't worry about me, Hoss, when it's my time to go, it's my time."

The Nashville-bound group tried to stay behind the storm clouds because Randy was not an instrument pilot and had to navigate by watching the terrain beneath him. As they got into Tennessee, Randy could not find his way through the dense clouds they found themselves in so they landed in Dyersburg to let the storm clouds get ahead of them. They watched the clouds move east and, impatient to get home, they soon took off again despite the warnings of the Dyersburg Airport officials.

Somewhere over Camden, Tennessee, about ninty miles from home, their small plane was swallowed up by the black storm clouds. They crashed in the West Tennessee hills that border the Tennessee River. There were no survivors.

Dottie was mowing grass in her yard one day, when she got a telephone call. "Dottie, I would like to record you — when do you think we might be able to get together about it?" said a man's soft voice. It was Chet Atkins, a record producer for RCA Victor who is credited with developing the Nashville Sound that was shaped in the 1950s, a smooth, calculating music marked by string instruments. The Nashville Sound superseded the honky-tonk sound of the 1940s that introduced electric guitars, piano and drums to country music.

Atkins, the most recorded instrumentalist of all time, joined the Grand Ole Opry in 1950. In the late 1940s, he had played guitar and fiddle behind Red Foley, the Carter Sisters and Mother Maybelle. By 1950, he had become the top session guitarist in Nashville.

Atkins had heard about Dottie West from Nashville songwriter Hank Cochran and an East Texas singer he was recording on RCA, Jim Reeves.

A short time later, Bill and Dottie bought their first home. Now Dottie's dreams were being realized.

Jean McDaniel had moved out of town

and Dottie missed her babysitter and close friend very much. However, Mr. West, Bill's daddy had passed away, leaving Mrs. West free to care for the children.

The West family luckily woke up one night just in time to get out of their burning home. They were not able to save anything except the clothes on their backs. For a few days Dottie felt like her dreams had gone up in that smoke. She thought of all her beautiful silver and china she had lost. She had hardly used the china, afraid of chipping or breaking it, but now it was all gone.

Bill and Dottie began looking for another house. They found one in Greenhills, across town from where their first home was located. The second house was much larger and closer to Music Row but Dottie said she would always hold her first house dear to her heart. A long time after the fire, she would wake up during the night and listen for the sound of crackling and roaring of fire. It was going to take time, but Dottie had learned to be a strong person throughout her life. Again, she would bounce back.

She began writing songs for Tree Publishing Company with buddies Willie Nelson, Roger Miller, and Hank Cochran. Her first songwriting effort, "Is This Me," became a chart-topper for her friend, Jim Reeves, in 1963.

Dottie joined the Grand Ole Opry as a regular in 1963, bringing to reality the fantasies of a little Tennessee girl who walked the hills and hollows selling Rosebud Salve to neighbors to get her first guitar.

Then began the glory days for Dottie West. For the next three decades, she would sing her heart out and win everything from the coveted Grammy Award to trade awards, as well as BMI awards for her songwriting. She would write more than four hundred songs, keep up a schedule of more than two hundred concerts a year, appear in movies and theatrical productions, and continue playing the Grand Ole Opry on Saturday night.

A number one hit, "Here Comes My Baby," which Dottie wrote with her husband and recorded for RCA, garnered her the National Academy of Recording Arts and Sciences Award in April, 1965 for best female vocal performer. The NARAS Award, called a Grammy, was the first ever given to a woman in country music.

The NARAS Grammy is equivalent to a movie Oscar award.

The night that Dottie received the Grammy was the same night that her friend,

Roger Miller received five Grammy awards, for his hit song "Dang Me." Miller grabbed every award in every division of the country and western division that night except best female vocal performer, which Dottie won. The only other Nashville-connected award in the forty-six NARAS categories that year went to Tennessee Ernie Ford and the Jordanaries for their best gospel recording, "Great Gospel Songs."

Dottie was to follow that triumph with more than two dozen Top 40 hits over the next ten years. Solo smashes like "Would You Hold It Against Me" and "Paper Mansions" were Top 10 hits.

Dottie also received an award for Best Vocalist in the country and western field at a presentation in Phoenix, Arizona, at the International Western Market Pioneer Awards Ball.

In 1966, to meet the demands of a heavy personal appearance schedule, Dottie formed a new band she named "The Heartaches," with Bill West backing her on his steel guitar as he had since their college days. Other members of the band were Bob Taylor, Ray Wix and Danny Shannon.

In addition to performing at coliseums, auditoriums and state fairs across the country, Dottie and her band headlined shows frequently at the Black Poodle Club and the Captain's Table in Nashville's famous Printers Alley, and she packed them in at The Roof, a nightclub on the top of Roger Miller's King of the Road Motor Inn in Nashville.

On April 21, 1967, late in the afternoon, Dottie was getting ready to be on the Opry when the phone rang. The person on the other end of the line informed her that her daddy had passed away that afternoon. Dottie was filled with mixed emotions. She had not seen him in eighteen years when she had faced him in court. Dottie went on to the Opry, shaken and nervous, however, keeping the news to herself. The next few days she was filled with emotional feelings, but she could not turn back the pages of her life and change a thing. A few days later, Hollis was buried in the New Union Cemetery in DeKalb County. His grave is only a few feet away from the fenced-in area of where his father-in-law, Bill Jones, is buried.

There were now two performances of the Opry on both Friday and Saturday nights, but the old Ryman still could not hold the crowds that wanted to come. The decision was made to move to a new location on Briley Parkway out of the downtown area. Construction of the new Grand Ole Opry House began on November 12, 1971. The goal of WSM officials and architects was to build an auditorium that would maintain the intimacy of the performers and their audience in this first building that was built specifically as a home for the Grand Ole Opry.

The Grand Ole Opry House, which can seat 4,400 people, is one of the largest auditoriums in the nation and is the largest radio and television broadcasting studio in the world. It also is the focal anchor of a country music theme park, Opryland U.S.A., and next door is the luxurious Opryland Hotel.

Inset in the center of the maple hardwood stage of the new auditorium is a disc of oak flooring, six feet in diameter, from the stage of the old Ryman Auditorium.

Dottie often said that every time she stood on that special spot in front of the mike, she thought of all the people who had stood on that very piece of wood before her, like the evangelist Sam Jones and famous singers like Hank Williams and Red Foley.

Dottie performed on the Opry that last night at the Ryman, Friday, March 15, 1974. She was on stage the very next night at the first performance in the new Grand Ole

Opry House. In the audience that night was President Richard M. Nixon. Indeed, the little girl born in a log cabin in Bain Hollow in Middle Tennessee had come a long way.

However, a great burden weighed heavily on Dottie's shoulders at this time. Her mother had been having strokes for the past year and everything the doctors did was not helping. Dottie called home one morning and was told to fly in at once. Her mother was seriously ill. The next morning, Pelina died in Dottie's arms. Dottie realized that she had lost her greatest friend. It seemed that everyone whom Pelina had ever done a good deed for during their time of sorrow wanted to pay their respects. It was said to be one of the largest funerals ever in McMinnville. Dottie pushed herself right back into her work to help her get over her loss.

But Dottie was in for another loss. Her marriage to Bill was ending in a divorce. It was a loss to all of Dottie's people. They had grown to love Bill dearly.

Not too much time had passed when she married again to a man by the name of Barron Metcalf. Nine years later, it too, ended in divorce.

Dottie decided it was time to move. Only this time, it was a mansion on forty acres of beautiful rolling land. Her people were over-joyed. They thought she was settling down to retire. For years, they had begged her to slow down. "But I can't," she would say. "When I'm booked, I have to be there."

Dottie, unlike most country music stars, continued to play the Nashville night club scene throughout most of her career. Her booking agent, Jack Andrews, vice president of Moeller Talent, told a *Nashville Banner* en-tertainment writer in 1974 that Dottie West was one of about three country music enter-tainers in demand in the Nashville area.

"There is only a handful of country per-formers capable of drawing good audiences in this city," Andrews said, "and it's due pri-marily to their up-town-type shows. Most people here don't really go in for country music stage performances. It's strange, but true."

"Country Sunshine" was a spin-off of a Coca-Cola commercial that won her a Clio Award. Dottie also had a great number-one record in 1980, "A Lesson in Leavin'," and she hit the top of the charts several times as Kenny Rogers' 1978-81 singing partner on

songs such as "Every Time Two Fools Col-
lide," "Anyone Who Isn't Me Tonight," "All I
Ever Need Is You," "Til I Can Make It on My
Own" and "What Are We Doin' in Love." Earlier, she also had notable success as the
duet partner of Jimmy Dean, Don Gibson,
and Jim Reeves.

The girl who was born in a cabin in a hollow in Middle Tennessee and never had
enough to eat as she was growing up, would
see the day in the 1990s, when she was
nearly sixty years old, that she could make
from $5,000 to $10,000 for a concert, and
could still line up more than eighty concerts
a year.

McMinnville had established "Dottie West
Day," an annual event when the town would
honor the person city officials called "Warren County's brightest star in the singing
and recording field." That first big day in
1965 attracted more than 10,000 visitors to
the small Middle Tennessee city, including
some from as far away as the western
United States and Canada.

Riding in the parade through downtown
that afternoon and appearing with the guest

of honor in the country music show that night at the city's stadium, were big-name Grand Ole Opry stars Chet Atkins, the Wilburn Brothers, Bobby Lord, Minnie Pearl, and Carl Perkins.

"I remember small things about Dot Marsh," said Nancy Wright, a teacher at Warner Elementary School in Nashville, who lived in the same college dormitory with the future country music star. "Like when Dot dumped a whole bottle of Clorox into a load of wash and ruined the load of clothes."

Wright said she remembered Dot as "a busy person," who, despite her studies and her numerous extracurricular activities, found time to iron for the other women in the dormitory. She apparently never thought of charging for the service. "I remember that when Dot had a chance to iron, she actually enjoyed it," Wright said, "Friends were delighted to have Dot press their clothes." Wright and others in the dormitory did not know that Dot had grown up without running water, electricity or modern appliances, and that she delighted in being able to use them.

A neighbor in the married students' housing also found out that Dot was willing to wash dishes and clean up a kitchen for her friends.

"She invites Bill and me to come to dinner but when we get there, all her dirty dishes and pots and pans are stacked in the sink. I have to wash them before she can fix dinner and we can eat," Dot told another neighbor. "Sometimes I think she just invites us when all her dishes need washing and her kitchen needs cleaning up."

ELEVEN

Country Sunshine

By the time Dottie was in her fifties, most of her dreams of fame, fortune and the good life had come true.

She was making from $1 to $2 million a year with record sales and keeping up a heavy road schedule. She was living in a colonial mansion on forty acres of prime farmland in Williamson County just outside of Nashville with her third husband, a man twenty-two years younger than she.

With all that Dottie achieved in life and with all of the traveling she did, she never forgot the hard times of growing up. There were things that happened that she would have liked to forget, yet so many of her childhood memories she held dear to her heart.

On the land surrounding her mansion

are signs that she indeed, was raised on country sunshine. Her flower and herb gardens are reminders that she still found time from her busy schedule to work in the soil.

In Dottie's heart she was born a country girl and she would die a country girl.

The little girl who didn't see her first movie until she was twelve years old now had appeared in a movie and in a stage production.

For four weeks in the summer of 1982, Dottie played the role of the madam in "The Best Little Whorehouse in Texas" on the stage in Ohio and Michigan, and early in 1983, she played the role in productions in Miami, Birmingham, Memphis, and Hawaii.

Then in 1984, she made her dramatic film debut in the movie, *Aurora Encounter*, which was based on the true story of an encounter with extra-terrestrial life by citizens in the small town of Aurora, Texas.

The film by New World Pictures was directed by Jim McCullough and starred Jack Elam and Mickey Hayes, a youth who had the "aging disease," as a space alien. It was an interesting picture, but not a box office smash.

Also, the aspiring young singer from McMinnville, who lived for the opportunity to go to Nashville to see the Grand Ole Opry, now was admired and loved by fans all over the world as one of the top country singers and songwriters. She had performed in auditoriums, clubs, and state fairs all across this country and in several foreign countries, including England and Saudi Arabia.

She had appeared on numerous network television shows, including a leading role in *The Love Boat,* as well as *Austin City Limits, Hee Haw, Family Feud,* and *Entertainment Tonight,* and most of the television programs originating in Nashville, including *Nashville Now* and *Crook and Chase.*

She had had her own float in Macy's Thanksgiving Day Parade in New York City and had been grand marshal of the Nashville Christmas Parade. She was called on frequently to donate her time to charitable causes promoted by society matrons of Nashville.

And she appeared often at the Warren County Fair in her hometown of McMinnville, Tennessee, usually inviting her nine siblings, all of whom still lived in Warren County, to join her on stage when she was performing.

"I actually do believe that dreams really do come true," Dottie told an interviewer on the national televised program, *Lifestyles of the Rich and Famous.* The television crew was filming a day in the life of Dottie and her family at her Williamson County showplace.

"I never thought I would go to places I've been,"she said. "I never thought I would go to Saudi Arabia — I never thought I would go to Peoria, Illinois — I only wanted to go to Nashville — seventy-two miles away."

The camera zoomed in on the dining table set for a formal dinner in the elegant dining room, the expensive china, crystal, and silverware reflecting the light from the brilliant chandelier overhead.

Dottie said she did not put her best linens and dishes up just to be used on special occasions. She learned to use them after her home in East Nashville had burned in 1969, destroying everything the family had, including Dottie's collection of fine dining pieces.

"I had the linens, the china, the crystal then and I didn't use them and everything was destroyed," she said. "So I say use them all the time."

Perhaps in Dottie's mind was the reflection of the lard bucket lids and tin cans that graced the rough dining table of her childhood.

In the television special, Dottie, attired in a dress reminiscent of the Old South, and husband, Alan Winters, posed on an upstairs balcony with the rolling Middle Tennessee hills as a backdrop. The couple snuggled in a white, lacy hammock on the lush green lawn as the cameras rolled.

Also for the cameras, Dottie glided down the ornate staircase of the entrance hallway of her four-level home and sent the pins flying in the bowling alley in her basement.

Glimpses were given to television viewers of her lavishly furnished boudoir with the mirrored ceiling and her closets filled with designer clothes.

There was even the "fairy tale" nursery she had designed in her home for her two granddaughters. She enjoyed having Tess Marie, daughter of Shelly and her first husband, Allen Frizzel, and Dorothy May, the daughter of Dottie's oldest child, Morris, visit her when she was not on the road.

Telling how hard she had worked to achieve her success, Dottie perhaps came closer on this television special to revealing the hard truth of her deprived childhood to the public than ever before. Often on television, she was introduced as a country girl who had grown up working hard.

"If you could see where I came from, where I lived as a child and how I lived," she said in a voice cracking with emotion. "Po' ain't the word for it," she finished, falling

back into the colloquialisms of her childhood.

Recalling that her mother had died at the
age of fifty-three, the age Dottie was now,
she said she had learned that life is short
and that "you should live all you can, be
happy and help others."

Ironically, Dottie was speaking words of
prophecy. The storm clouds were rolling
back into her life and just ahead were dark
days.

TWELVE

The Walls Come Tumbling Down

Her tears and her humiliation were on national television for all to see. Dottie West, who had made millions in her thirty-year singing career, was broke. "I never thought it would come to this, I thought I could handle it, I thought I could pay," she said with tears streaking her cheeks as she faced the television cameras in her luxurious four-level home near Nashville.

Wearing jeans and a tee-shirt and no makeup, she looked more like the abused country girl she had been than the sophisticated entertainer she had become. The camera crew of *Entertainment Tonight* was filming as she sat on a couch in her living room with a stunned look on her face. Boxes filled with her belongings were sitting throughout the house.

It was August, 1990. She owed the Internal Revenue Service $1.3 million, which was due in September. A West Coast management firm was suing her for $130,000, alleging breach of contract. Her former manager, Michael Brokaw, was suing her for $110,-295, which he claimed was his 15 percent of her earnings he had been promised but not paid. The bank had repossessed her Corvette automobile. Adding to all of this was the fact that Dottie had fallen behind on her mortgage payments.

First American National Bank bought the $1.6 million Williamson County mansion and the approximate forty acres of rolling farmland that surrounded it, at public auction for $800,000 in June. An eviction order was filed against Dottie on August 1, when she still had not moved out.

And if that were not enough, she and her third husband, Allen Winters, had divorced in January and he was now suing her for $7,500.

Dottie was fifty-seven years old.

She told the *Entertainment Tonight* interviewer that she had had the same business manager from 1976 to 1985 and that he had made some bad investments. That was when her career as at its height. The interviewer identified the business manager as Al Mifflin of Nashville.

"He called me one morning and told me I was the new owner of three Italian-built tuna boats," Dottie told the interviewer. "I found out later the boats had never even been built." She also pointed out that she was so busy with her career that she didn't have time to keep up with her finances.

Relatives and friends who had known Dottie since her childhood knew that she had started out making a few dollars picking beans and peas on neighbors' farms. Then later, she barely got by financially with four small children when she began her career. And finally, to making millions when she reached her peak. She had not had time along the way to learn to manage money.

But Dottie's mettle had been tempered in the flames and she wasn't melting now.

When her home was sold at the auction, Dottie stood with the small group of lawyers and businessmen around the courthouse steps as the auctioneer sang out the funeral knell for her beloved home: "Going once, going twice, and this property has been sold."

Dottie, wearing a red jacket and dark

glasses showed little emotion as her dreams came tumbling down around her.

As she faced the *Entertainment Tonight* cameras and reporters two months later, she vowed she would go back on the road and make more money.

"I never thought it would come to this, but they can't take my songs and they can't take my soul," she said. "I've learned a lot from this and I know that this too shall pass."

In mid-August, the country music luminary filed for bankruptcy in the United States Bankruptcy Court in Nashville, citing more than $1 million in debts. She filed under Chapter 11, which allows for consolidation and reorganization after filing for bankruptcy.

Included were at least twenty other creditors in addition to the Internal Revenue Service such as First American National Bank, Williamson County, Sovran Bank, Third National Bank, Neiman-Marcus, Dearborn & Ewing law firm, Ford Credit Company, Brentwood Limousines, and American Express.

She estimated the worth of her personal items at $200,000. Later she converted to Chapter 7 bankruptcy which allows for liquidation. She changed the estimation of her personal possessions to $50,000.

Dottie had vowed she would keep going and she did. Offers of financial assistance came from several professional agencies, but like her mother, Pelina, who had been too proud to turn to relatives or accept charity, Dottie found the strength within herself to go on.

She moved to the Wessex Towers Condominiums on Nashville's west side. When her car was repossessed, her old friend and singing partner, Kenny Rogers, gave her a three-year-old car, which she used to get around town.

She was playing the Grand Ole Opry, often performing at the 8:30 and 11:00 segments on both Friday and Saturday nights. And she was on the road again, with eighty concert dates already lined up. Just one month's bookings would take her to Minnesota, Branson, Missouri, Rhode Island, New York, Maine, Ohio, and South Carolina.

Industry sources estimated that she would make from $5,000 to $10,000 a concert.

"I'm a survivor," Dottie told Robert K. Oermann, a reporter for *The Tennessean*, Nashville's morning newspaper.

"I know how to make money and I'll make it," she declared.

When her back was to the wall, Dottie West's instinct for survival kicked in.

The story broke March 27, 1991, in the *Nashville Banner*, the city's afternoon newspaper.

"Bankrupt singer's valuables hidden?" asked the headline to reporter Leslie McCullough's story revealing that bankruptcy trustee John C. McLemore believed that Dottie may have stashed china, crystal, porcelain, Oriental rugs, paintings, and other expensive items to protect them from being auctioned by the court. McLemore said he had been informed that at least one rental truck load of boxes was taken from Dottie's Williamson County home. They had been taken to a Store-N-Lok facility in Nashville. That was shortly before a moving company van arrived at the house to move the bankrupt country music star's possessions to her newly rented Nashville condominium.

Two days later, McLemore, with reporters in tow, opened two storage warehouses on Trousdale Avenue that were filled with boxes variously marked "D.W.," "D.W. videos," "stage clothes," "china," "silver closet," and "Xmas items." As several boxes were opened to assess their contents, one item of particular note that was found was a Spanish porcelain statue, which Nashville jewelers estimated could be worth from $2,000 to $6,000. Also discovered was a Tiffany lamp, causing McLemore to exclaim, "If it's a real Tiffany lamp, that's big bucks."

The contents of the rental storage warehouses were moved to an undisclosed place where bankruptcy officials and an auctioneer could inventory the goods and ready them for auction.

The next week the other shoe fell.

Bankruptcy officials had visited Dottie in her second-floor condominium on March 13 in hopes of finding valuable items, particularly crystal and silver, that she had not reported in her bankruptcy petition and which could be sold to help pay the nearly $1.5 million she owed the IRS and about $900,-000 she owed other creditors.

After they discovered the storage warehouses, bankruptcy officials were tipped off again. This time they learned that furniture and other items had been removed from the singer's condominium the night before they paid their visit.

They returned to Wessex Towers and asked for the key to the tenth floor, where Dottie had hidden some of her precious possessions.

The discovery of the two storage warehouses and the tenth floor condominium produced 450 boxes and twenty-five large crates of valuables.

But the searchers couldn't find her silver and crystal collection.

Then the FBI entered the picture, looking for possible criminal violations of the National Bankruptcy Act because of Dottie's attempts to conccal property.

The property seized by bankruptcy officials was auctioned off on June 13 and 14 at a warehouse on Elm HIll Pike. The sale was held during Fan Fair Week, the time when thousands of country music fans visit Nashville to meet the stars and take part in lavish festivities.

Being the trouper that she was, Dottie went to the auction, talked to the buyers, and bid on some of her own stuff.

Some of her fans bought a number of her prized porcelain dolls and returned them to her.

Items sold included a white baby grand piano that went for $4,900. Many things brought far less than auctioneers had anticipated, such as a 1976 black Fleetwood Cadillac that went for $3,100, a brass canopy bed that brought $1,700, and a large china cabinet that sold for $1,600.

Bill Colson, owner of Bill Colson Auction and Realty Company, Inc., called the auction a success since many of the singer's personal items drew large bids from Fan Fair attendees looking for souvenirs. But it didn't get Dottie West out of debt.

A little over a month later—July 20—Dottie was slightly injured in a one-car accident as she was driving to the Grand Ole Opry. She was treated at Baptist Hospital for a laceration on her nose from the accident that happened about 9:20 p.m. She had lost control of the 1991 Chevrolet Camaro convertible she was driving and crashed into a concrete wall.

The singer was ticketed for careless driving and not wearing a seatbelt. She also was issued a citation for driving with an expired temporary tag. She told police an auto dealership was allowing her to use the car. Metro traffic investigator, Brad Putnam, told a *Tennessean* reporter that Dottie West was in good spirits following the ordeal. When she signed the police citations, she asked the officer, "This isn't nothing that I'm signing for the IRS, is it?"

THIRTEEN

The Lord Lifted Me

When Dottie was growing up in rural Warren County, church attendance was important to her mother. Pelina got the children up on Sunday mornings and walked to the Baptist Church at Moore's College. The children who weren't big enough to walk to the church stayed home with Hollis.

As she got older, Dottie often attended the Bluff Springs Church of Christ with the W.E. Morgan family that lived across the field from the Marshes. This was the family that also hired Dottie and Pelina to work in the fields. She could ride in a car to church when she went with the Morgans.

But her attendance at church was rare after she left Warren County to go to college.

When she was fifty-eight years old and her world came crashing down around her,

18

COUNTRY SUNSHINE

she must have felt the need in her life for the comfort and love of a higher power.

On Easter, 1991, she attended an Easter drama at the Abundant Life Church in Mt. Juliet, a small town near Nashville. Her son, Kerry, who traveled with her on the road as her sound equipment manager, was active in this congregation and tonight he was portraying Jesus in the Easter drama.

At the close of the drama, the Rev. Ray Hughes gave an invitation for all "who wanted to invite the Lord into their lives" to walk down the aisle to the front of the auditorium. Softly strumming a guitar, he implored those who were not in a relationship with God to lift their hands.

Then he urged them to come forward. He sang a simple tune as he strummed the guitar:

> "Oh, the blood of Jesus,
> "Oh, the blood of Jesus,
> "Oh, the blood of Jesus, it washes
>   white as snow."

"Does anybody need a special touch from the Lord tonight?" he coaxed. "I feel like the Lord wants to make sure we all leave here as white as snow."

A few people came forward and stood in front of the minister. Then Dottie West, dressed in a white suit, came slowly down the aisle leaning heavily on the arm of her son, Kerry, who was still dressed in the white robe he had worn as Jesus in the drama.

The minister prayed for all who had come forward. Then placing his hand on each penitent sinner, prayed a personal prayer.

Moving to Dottie, he said joyfully, "God bless you, Dottie!"

Then with a hand on her shoulder, he prayed, "Lord I lift Kerry and his mother up to You. We bring Dottie to the Lord. No, she brings herself to You, she loves You and she has chosen You. She has chosen this night for You to touch her in ways she has never been touched on this earth." The minister beseeched God "to do something so deep and so special in her heart and in her life that the enemy will not be able to rob her anymore and destroy her."

He said that Satan had come to steal Dottie, to rob her, to create havoc in her life and to bring hurt to her life. "I pray that You will put a new song on her lips and a new song in her heart this night, one that only You could write and only You could sing," the minister prayed. "Lord, sing through this daughter of Zion from this day forward."

Placing his arms around both Dottie and Kerry, Hughes thanked God for "welding this family together," and said that with the power and authority of God serving as the glue to bind them together, "nothing on earth or in hell can destroy what You are doing tonight."

Laying his hand on Kerry's shoulder, Hughes prayed, "Lord, I thank you for redeeming everything that has been lost in Kerry's life down through the years."

Then the minister led the small group gathered around the altar in a prayer of confession:

"Dear Lord Jesus, I come to You as a sinner. I ask You to forgive me for my sins, cleanse me from all unrighteousness, but most of all, forgive me of my sins I have confessed tonight."

As the penitents turned to face the congregation, Kerry West took the microphone from the minister and made his own public confession. "Tonight, everyone of you has been touched," he said to the congregation. "You all have looked at me and wondered where this fellow has come from." In a voice shaking with emotion, he told them that he was "a product of Mom and Dad." He said he was blessed with a mother and father who had shown him great love."I thank the Lord up above for such a blessed Mom and Dad," he said.

Dottie told the minister that she always wanted to dance with the angels and sing with the angel band.

Six months later, country music star Dottie West would be dead.

On the evening of August 30, 1991, Dottie was leaving her home in the Wessex Towers to drive to the Grand Ole Opry House. She was having trouble starting her borrowed car, and George Thackston, eighty-one, another resident of the condominium, assisted her.

However, the car later stalled in front of the old Belle Meade Theater on Harding Road. Wearing her stage clothes and frantic to get to her job on time, she flagged a passing motorist.

The motorist turned out to be George, and he agreed to drive her to the Opry House.

Trying to make up for lost time, George accelerated the car to 55 mph on an Opryland entrance ramp, where the posted speed limit was only 25 mph. Dottie was to perform at 8:30 p.m. George lost control of his car at 8:11 p.m.

George's 1982 Plymouth Reliant left the roadway, going airborne and traveled 165 feet before striking the embankment of an exit ramp. Both Dottie and George were conscious when they were admitted to Vanderbilt University Medical Center.

George suffered leg, back and hip injuries, but eventually recovered. Dottie, however, was in critical condition. Kenny Rogers, Dottie's dear friend and former singing partner, visited her as doctors were preparing for surgery. Her liver had received multiple injuries that needed attention immediately. Rogers promised her they would record another song together after she recovered. She smiled at Rogers and whispered, "Thank you."

However, several deep lacerations to Dottie's liver could not be repaired in two early operations because she was bleeding too much, doctors said. In addition, Dottie's spleen was ruptured.

Dottie had lost tremendous amounts of blood, and had to be given a total of thirty-five units. Dr. John A. Morris, director of Vanderbilt's Trauma Center, said that even with today's technology a person of nearly sixty years old would have a difficult time surviving such blood loss.

Fifty-eight-year-old Dottie's heart stopped

on the operating table. She was pronounced dead from heart failure at 9:43 a.m.

When the news of Dottie West's death hit the newspapers and airwaves, family, friends, colleagues, and fans across the nation were grief-stricken.

"The last two days, I have absorbed so much love, from people who were very close to my mother, from people who met her, and from people who just loved her singing," Shelly West told reporters at a press conference at Nashville's Woodlawn Funeral Home the day following her mother's death. "At the same time, I've been able to exchange that love. I tried to let them recognize the love that she had for them also."

Woodlawn official Ken Lee Jr. said the funeral home had been inundated with phone calls and flowers. He said floral arrangements had been received from virtually every country music star.

"Because of Dottie West's death, the country sunshine is not so bright today," wrote a *Tennessean* editorialist.

Hundreds of mourners—country music performers, music industry professionals, and even a congressman — mingled with Dottie's fans in the sancturary of Christ Church on Old Hickory Boulevard in Nashville. A memorial service had been held in the same church for Reba McEntire's band members who had been killed in a plane crash.

A simple song of love, written and recorded by Dottie's granddaughters, Tess Marie Frizzel and Dorothy Mae West, was played:

> *Dottie, oh Dottie, we love you so*
> *Dottie, oh Dottie, we didn't want to*
>   *let you go*
> *We love you and miss you Dottie*

The funeral procession left the Nashville church and wound its way down Interstate 24 to McMinnville, where Dottie was buried beside her mother in a private ceremony at Mount View Cemetery.

"She said she always wanted to dance with the angels and sing with the angel band," Reverend Hughes had said at the service. "Family, it's happening today."

F O U R T E E N

Epilogue

Dottie West brought a lot of country sun-shine to millions across our globe.

There was never a place too small or too large for her to entertain in. With her smiles and singing, she touched the lives of many and filled their hearts with hope for a new tomorrow.

No matter how far away Dottie went, she always spoke of her beloved hometown, McMinnville, Tennessee.

After the terrible heartbreak of losing Dottie, the citizens of McMinnville and other states expressed, with great honor, their love and respect for Dottie.

People from other states still visit her graveside and bring flowers.

Now on her birthday, October 11, her

grave is covered with flowers that have letters, cards, and poems attached to them.

The little country girl who never had a birthday party until she was seventeen, is now especially remembered on her birthday.

On July 13, 1993, a ceremony was held in McMinnville to dedicate Highway 56 from the McMinnville city limits to DeKalb County as the Dottie West Memorial Highway.

"We just want the world to know that this is the hometown of Dottie West," spoke County Commissioner Bill Zechman. Mayor Norman Rore spoke at the dedication. He informed the people that he was going to hold a meeting with the McMinnville Board of Mayor and Aldermen asking them to join him in seeing if the state would erect another sign naming Highway 56 inside the city limits Dottie West Boulevard. The mayor also knew Dottie well. They both attended McMinnville High School at the same time.

Barbara Taylor, president of the Downtown Business Association, spoke of the plans she and others had of organizing a Dottie West Festival. The festival would be held in downtown McMinnville each year to pay tribute to their friend Dottie. With great esteem, several other people spoke at the ceremony. Their admiration for Dottie was heartwarming.

That day, there was not a rain cloud in the sky. It was filled with beautiful country sunshine.

On all the major highways leading into McMinnville are signs that read:

McMinnville
Home of Grand Ole Opry Star
Dottie West

ORDER FORM

Use this form to order additional copies of
Country Sunshine
The Dottie West Story
for your friends or family members.

Name: _____

Address: _____

City: _____ St:____ Zip: _____

Daytime phone: (_____)_____

    If gift, message that you would like enclosed: _____

    _____

    _____

    _____

    If gift, ship to:

    Name _____

    Address: _____

    City: _____ St:____ Zip: _____

Method of Payment: *(Make payable to **Eggman Publishing, Inc.**)*
    ❑ Check   ❑ Money Order   ❑ VISA   ❑ MasterCard

Card# _____ Exp. _____

Signature: _____
      Required for credit card purchases

Quantity: _____ x $12.95 = $_____

Shipping & Handling Quantity: _____ x $ 2.00 = $_____

Sub Total: $_____

TN residents add 8.25% sales tax $_____

Total: $_____

Please return form and payment to: **Eggman Publishing, Inc.**
                                       3012 Hedrick Street
                                       Nashville, TN 37203

FOR FASTER SERVICE CALL 1–800–396–4626

Thank You!
Your order will be shipped within 1-3 weeks from receipt